CUSTOMER REVIEWS

"I'm new to juicing. I appreciate all the nutritional information within each recipe, i.e.: calories, salt, fiber, fat, carbs, protein etc. I decided (and was told) to start drinking smoothies for health reasons, and was surprised you can actually make tasty green smoothies?! Very nice surprise. Nicely designed cookbook, easy and simple to use." - Karen O.

"Juicing looked intimidating to me so I bought this book along with my blender. I was pleasantly surprised to see good instructions and tips for making smoothies 'like a pro'. Well, it worked. I'm excited about improving my diet and also having the occasional splurge." – Cathy J.

"We're finding many delicious recipes in this book. Easy to follow instructions got me up and running quickly. Thumbs up." – Tom B.

"The recipes here are well thought out with proper portions that fit the machine. I had trouble re: sizes with another book. This one has a variety of things I can make so I'm satisfied. I had never bought an appliance like this but saw a demonstration of all it could do and knew it had potential. This book brought it together. Thank you." -Erica A.

"This product continues to surprise us. We had no idea a blender could make such a wide variety of dishes. Very happy with this cookbook and certainly can recommend it. Simple, no nonsense layout. We're learning a lot and looking forward to more surprises." -Jason M.

LEGAL NOTICE

PAN PACIFIC PRESS

Published in the United States of America by Pan Pacific Press

www.Pan-PacificPress.com

Want a FREE Cookbook?

Then join the
Book Review Club!

(It's Free for readers like you)

Get your first free cookbook today
at this link:

www.JoinTheBookReviewClub.com/e2

TABLE OF CONTENTS

SOUPS   99

QUICK BREADS   115

PANCAKES AND WAFFLES   125

1

WHY YOU NEED THIS BOOK!

Get Started Right Now with Our Simple Illustrated Instructions

Congratulations on your purchase of The Magic Bullet blender system. As you may already be aware, The Magic Bullet is the most convenient home blending system on the market and our easy to follow, in depth instructions teach you everything you need to know in order to become a blending master in no time. From becoming familiar with The Magic Bullet's easy to use controls, to the suggestions about the best way to get amazing results, to properly cleaning and storing your Magic Bullet, this guide will provide you with everything you need to know to use your Magic Bullet confidently and safely. So lets get started by exploring all of the ways you can use your Magic Bullet to make the world's best smoothies, and so much more!

Get the Most from Your Magic Bullet with This In-Depth Guide

By now you probably know that you can make your own smoothies at home, but did you know that you can also make soups, pancake batter, cocktails and even peanut butter with The Magic Bullet? This in depth guide will teach you plenty of exciting ways to turn your favorite ingredients into healthy and delicious drinks and dishes, but you will also learn valuable techniques for how to get the absolute most out of your Magic Bullet. From choosing the best items to blend, to learning how to best fill The Magic Bullet blending cups, we take all of the guess work out of making amazing drinks and meals that will delight the entire family. In addition to easy to follow instructions and tips, we will also explore the science and history of blending to give you an understanding of all of the benefits of using The Magic Bullet. And did you know making your own smoothies is an amazing way to save money? This book will show you ways to get the most out of your ingredients so you can really see the savings.

Amazing Pro Tips for Making All Kinds of Smoothies, Pancakes, Sauces, Soups etc.

Once you've learned the basics of blending it's time to become a pro. This book will teach you everything you need to know to take your blending game to the next level with tips developed to maximize your results. Most people buy blenders to make smoothies and other types of blended drinks, but did you know that you can use your Magic Bullet to make pancakes, waffles, savory sauces, soups, and even delicious homemade peanut butter? Our vital pro tips will teach you to go beyond smoothies to help you get the absolute most out of your Magic Bullet. Once you've learned about all of the amazing things your Magic Bullet can do, you will wonder how you ever got by without one.

100 Amazing Recipes You Won't Find Anywhere Else!

Your Magic Bullet is perfect for making blended classics like smoothies and juices, but our exciting and diverse recipes go far beyond traditional recipes, providing you with endless possibilities for amazing beverages, soups, sauces, desserts, and even nut butters and baked goods! With so many unique recipes not found anywhere else, this guide will be a valuable tool as you navigate the wide world of blended treats. We will even give you step by step instructions on how to blend frozen fruit to make delicious desserts like sorbet, and nutritious homemade bread dough, which are great for the whole family because they contain no preservatives, added sugar, or harmful dyes and chemicals. This is truly the only guide you will ever need for using The Magic Bullet.

Avoid Common Mistakes and Become a Magic Bullet Pro!

The Magic Bullet is the easiest to use blender on the market today, but if you've never used a blender before, getting started might seem a little challenging. Luckily, this guide will show you how to avoid common mistakes and put you on a path to being a Magic Bullet expert in no time. The Magic Bullet is so convenient and so compact, you will find that there are a multitude of different tasks it can handle with ease, and we will teach you how to get the most out of your Magic Bullet. We will also teach you the best methods for cleaning and storing The Magic Bullet to improve your chances of getting perfect results for many years to come.

2

THE WONDERFUL WORLD OF THE MAGIC BULLET

What Separates The Magic Bullet from Other Blenders?

If you've purchased The Magic Bullet you may have done some research on the blenders currently on the market. Unlike many other blenders, The Magic Bullet has some unique features which set it apart from anything else out there. The Magic Bullet features the familiar blending cup technology which makes blending a breeze. Many people who chose The Magic Bullet do so because of the simple yet powerful design that has made The Magic Bullet one of the most popular blenders in the world. Because the cups are so compact, you can easily prepare unblended ingredients ahead of time and then blend whenever you want. This revolutionary design has many imitators, but the original Magic Bullet is optimized to be the highest performing blender in its class. The Magic Bullet also features a powerful 250 watt motor which gives you considerably more flexibility than other blenders because it can handle difficult to blend items like cubed ice, frozen fruit, and nuts. Once you've explored all of the amazing capabilities of your Magic Bullet, you will find you can blend virtually anything with ease.

A Brief History of Blenders

The blender has become a staple of the American kitchen, but blenders have been around for longer than you might think. All the way back in 1919, around the end of the first world war, the Stevens Electric Company began designing drink mixers because of the rising popularity of milkshakes at soda fountain counters. Over the next couple of decades different companies developed different drink mixer designs which solved a variety of problems that were plaguing soda jerks across the country. The first product called a "blender" was introduced in 1937 by Vitamix founder W.G. Bernhard, but it was still a fairly simple design which provided only an "on" and "off" function. By the 1960s blenders were becoming a more common item found in American households because the size of the units were becoming small enough that they could be efficiently stored. The rising popularity of blended drinks has only caused blenders to become more advanced and The Magic Bullet is an impressive step in the constant evolution of blending technology. A far cry from giant industrial models installed at soda counters, The Magic Bullet follows a proud tradition of blenders that offer greater control and versatility giving you the ability to get perfect results no matter what you need to blend.

Who Uses Magic Bullets?

If you love blended drinks, smooth batter, creamy soups, and delicious desserts that are cheaper and healthier than store bought foods, The Magic Bullet is for you. Store bought smoothies are expensive and are often loaded with extra sugar are artificial flavors. With your Magic Bullet you get to be in control of what goes into your drinks. You decide which fruits and vegetables go into your smoothies, and you can custom tailor the settings to get the perfect consistency from all of your blended foods. Many people these days are rightfully concerned about the dangers of added sugar in smoothies and other blended treats. The great thing about using The Magic Bullet is you get to control how much sugar is included. Now you can make smoothies that are healthier and packed with vital nutrients which other blenders can destroy. The Magic Bullet is also perfect for people on the go because of the unique blending cup technology. Simply fill the blending cups with your desired ingredients, blend with ease, and take the blending cup with you. The cups even have spout lids so you can take your smoothies in the car without worrying about spills.

What Kinds of Foods Can Be Prepared with The Magic Bullet?

The amazing thing about The Magic Bullet is the variety of different foods which can be blended with ease. Because The Magic Bullet features a powerful 250 watt motor, foods like frozen fruit can be effortlessly pureed in no time. The powerful motor, combined with The Magic Bullet's stainless steel cross blades means nearly anything you want to blend will come out perfectly and quickly. The Magic Bullet is designed to handle foods from fresh fruits and vegetables as well as nuts and seeds. It's also perfect for smooth blended cocktails that are perfect for entertaining. Once you start using your Magic Bullet you will quickly find that nearly anything can be easily chopped, ground, pureed or blended to perfection.

Helpful Accessories for Amazing Results

Your Magic Bullet comes with everything you need to get started right away, but let's go into a little more depth about the amazing accessories you get with your Magic Bullet. Your Magic Bullet comes with an eleven piece set that includes a tall cup, a short cup, a party mug, two comfort lip rings, two stay fresh resealable lids, and one flip top lid for convenience on the go. The blending cups are easy to take with you wherever you go and are made from the safest BPA free plastic. This ensures that your blending cups are not only safe to use, but also durable and long lasting. To make taking your blended beverages even easier, there is an included flip top lid which means you don't have to worry about making a mess on the go. The flip top lid is also perfect for the kids. You can also purchase additional blending cups so that there are enough for the entire family. The blending cups are available in a variety of sizes and colors.

Use Your Magic Bullet to Save Money!

These days it seems like everyone is looking for ways to save money when it comes to food. Did you know that about half of all produce grown in the United States every year is thrown away because of spoilage? That's 60 million tons of food that would have been worth $160 billion! Your Magic Bullet is a great way to save money by making sure you use all of the healthy produce you buy. Let's face it, getting kids to eat fruits and vegetables can be difficult, but making flavorful smoothies and other treats in your Magic Bullet means less produce is wasted. And because you can make so many different foods with your Magic Bullet, you can avoid paying high prices for prepackaged food at the market.

The Amazing Health Benefits of Using The Magic Bullet

The Magic Bullet is specifically designed to lock in the vital nutrients in the food you are blending. The Magic Bullet' simple press down mechanism is easy to use and takes all of the guess work out of blending your favorite foods, allowing you to preserve all of the vitamins and nutrients in your fresh food. In addition to preserving nutrition, The Magic Bullet promotes healthy eating by making blending fun. The whole family will be excited to try out different combinations of fruits, vegetables, nuts, and so much more. Instead of reaching for processed snacks and sugar filled drinks, encourage the whole family to get creative and come up with new and interesting healthy recipes. And because The Magic Bullet has such a powerful motor, you can easily process healthy greens into a fine and palatable puree. Other blenders can't handle hearty greens like kale and the result is chunky and stringy, but these types of greens are loaded with vital nutrients. The Magic Bullet makes quick work of these veggies for delightfully smooth smoothies every time.

3

HOW TO USE YOUR MAGIC BULLET BLENDER

Get Started in Minutes with This Easy Guide

Getting started with your Magic Bullet really couldn't be easier. Simply follow these steps and you will be on your way to blending in no time. First, remove The Magic Bullet from the box and remove all packing materials. Place the motor base on a flat, level surface. Make sure the motor base is plugged in before using. Wash and dry all of the blending cups before use. Place the ingredients you want to blend in the cup you would like to use. Each cup has a Max Fill line, and to ensure your Magic Bullet functions properly, it is important you do not overfill the cup. Once the cup is filled, screw on the blade cap until it is tight. Turn the cup over and place in onto the top of the motor base. Now, simply press down on the blending cup. This will activate the motor and blending will begin. When you stop pressing down on the cup, the motor will automatically turn off. If you want to blend for a longer period of time and don't want to press down the whole time, simply twist the cup to lock into place. When blending has finished, and the motor has come to a complete stop, pull the blending cup directly upward. It should easily detach from the base. Unscrew the blade cap from the cup and enjoy. You can store your blended foods in the blending cups, but do not store with the blade cap attached as this may cause damage to the blades. Screw the spout top onto the blending cup and you are ready to enjoy your blended drinks anywhere you go.

Master All the Controls and Settings in No Time

The Magic Bullet is designed to be as user friendly and simple as possible while still giving you state of the art features which will take the guess work out of your blending. Because there is no display, there is no confusion about how to get great results. All you need to do is fill your cup with your desired ingredients, screw on the blades, and press the cup onto the motor base. You decides exactly how long you want to blend, and the powerful motor and precise stainless steel blades do the rest. The Magic Bullet's cups even feature the patented Cyclonic Cutting Zone technology which allows for more efficient blending by allowing your ingredients to circulate more rapidly during the blending process.

Prepare Your Foods for The Magic Bullet

Depending on what you're going to be blending, you will want to do a little preparation before getting started. For fruits and vegetables, you will want to trim the stems and remove the seeds before blending. Since The Magic Bullet isn't a juicer it will not remove pulp or skin, so it is important to remove those parts of the fruits or vegetables before blending if you do not want them in your smoothie. If you are using The Magic Bullet to make nut butters, keep in mind that The Magic Bullet was not designed to blend completely dry ingredients so it is recommended that you add oil when blending items like nuts or seeds.

Important Safety Tips for Your Magic Bullet iQ

Because The Magic Bullet uses a stainless steel blade cap assembly, it is important to make sure you handle the blades as carefully as possible. Always be sure to hold the blades away from your body and never in close proximity to another person. When you are getting ready to blend, make sure that the blade cap is firmly screwed onto the blending cups. Before starting the motor, turn the blender cups slightly to ensure they are properly in place. An improperly installed blender cup can damage the cup or the motor. Before you remove the cup after blending, make sure the motor has come to a complete stop.

How to Clean and Store Your Magic Bullet

Always make sure to store your Magic Bullet unplugged and in a dry place. After blending, use a damp cloth to clean the exterior of the motor base and make sure no food or debris has fallen into the opening on top. Never submerge the motor base in water and never put in the dishwasher. The blending cups can be washed with soap and water, but for longer life, avoid washing in the dishwasher. Make sure to wash the blade assembly well between uses.

The Absolute Best Ways to Safely Store Your Prepared Meals

Since you can make so many different types of foods with your Magic Bullet, there are many great ways to store the foods you've made. For items like smoothies and batters, often the best method for storing is to use the blender cups provided with your Magic Bullet. They come in three convenient sizes and are BPA free so you don't have to worry about the possibility of harmful chemicals finding their way into your food. If you find that after storing a smoothie in the blender cup that the ingredients have begun to separate, simply screw on the blade cap and pulse for a few seconds on your Magic Bullet.

4

PRO TIPS

Use Your Magic Bullet for Condiments, Peanut Butter and More!

Many people buy The Magic Bullet because it is the perfect tool for making perfect smoothies, but it does so much more than that. You can make homemade mayonnaise and ketchup in seconds with your Magic Bullet. Perfectly blended salad dressing is made simple with a few pulses in your Magic Bullet, including getting a fine puree of anchovy for classic Caesar salad dressing. And believe it or not, The Magic Bullet is powerful enough to make nut butters. Now you can have healthy, all natural peanut butter with no added sugar or preservatives. Just add nuts and oil and blend to your desired consistency.

You Can Use Your Magic Bullet to Make Pizza Dough, Sorbets, Dips

The Magic Bullet is such a diverse appliance that you can even make bread and pizza dough with ease. The Magic Bullet's powerful motor and high quality blades take all of the guess work out of blending perfect doughs which can be used for pizza, bread, and crackers. You can also use your Magic Bullet to make amazingly smooth and decadent sorbets with fruits of your choice. In our recipes section we will give you more ideas for combining fruits to make delightful desserts which are sure to please the whole family. But that's not all! You can even make thick and creamy dips which are perfect for entertaining. Once you start using your Magic Bullet you will be astonished at how much you can do.

The Best Order for Stacking Food in Your Magic Bullet

If you are planning to use your Magic Bullet to blend different ingredients at the same time, you might be wondering if there is an ideal order to how to stack them in the blending cups. The answers is yes! Because the top of the cup is the part that will make contact with the blades first, you will want to put your hardest item in the cup last. That means if you want to have fruit, vegetables, and ice in your smoothie, try placing the vegetables in the cup first. Follow the vegetables with a layer of juicy fruit. At the very top of the cup place your ice. That way, the high speed blades will crush the ice first before getting to the juicy fruit and fresh vegetables. This will lead to easy and even blending.

How to Make Juice with Your Magic Bullet

While The Magic Bullet isn't technically a juicer, that doesn't mean you can't make juice with it. The high powered motor and precise blade assembly means maximum blending power. Once you've thoroughly pureed your ingredients, you are left with a mixture of juice and pulp which is the healthiest way to consume your fruits and vegetable because you get the nutrients as well as the beneficial fiber. If you don't want all that pulp, though, you can place a simple piece of cheesecloth over a bowl or pitcher and pour the puree over it. The juice will filter through into the bowl and you can discard the pulp. You now have perfectly fresh juice.

5

MAGIC BULLET RECIPES

Mango Banana Smoothie

This easy to make fruit smoothie is perfect for breakfast or after a long workout. You can also try substituting the frozen mango for other frozen fruit.

Prep time: 2 minutes

Cook time: 2 minutes

Servings: 2

Ingredients:

2 bananas, peeled

1 cup frozen mango chunks

3/4 cups plain or greek yogurt

1 cup orange juice

Instructions:

1. Place the bananas, mango, yogurt, and orange juice in the medium or large Magic Bullet blending cup. screw on the blade assembly and place the cup on the Magic Bullet. Press down to blend.

2. When the Magic Bullet is finished blending, pour the smoothie into two glasses and enjoy.

Nutritional Info: Calories: 293, Sodium: 61 mg, Dietary Fiber: 4.6 g, Fat: 1 g, Carbs: 56.7 g, Protein: 19.3 g.

Super Berry Smoothie

This refreshing berry smoothie is packed with antioxidants thanks to a big dose of blueberries and cherries. It's also bursting with flavor and is the perfect way to cool off on a hot summer day.

Prep time: 3 minutes

Cook time: 2 minutes

Servings: 4

Ingredients:

1 cup frozen strawberries

1 cup frozen blueberries

1 cup frozen cherries

1 cup frozen blackberries or raspberries

1 cup plain or greek yogurt

2/3 cups orange juice

1 banana, peeled

Instructions:

1. Place the frozen berries, banana, yogurt, and orange juice in the 32oz. Magic Bullet blending cup. Screw on the blade assembly and place the cup on the Magic Bullet. Press down to blend.

2. When the Magic Bullet is finished blending, pour the smoothie into four glasses and enjoy.

Nutritional Info: Calories: 149, Sodium: 18 mg, Dietary Fiber: 5 g, Fat: 7 g, Carbs: 29.3 g, Protein: 6.8 g.

Ginger Banana Smoothie

This flavorful combination is perfect for getting started in the morning because if combines vital nutrition found in bananas with the amazing powers of fresh ginger.

Prep time: 5 minutes

Cook time: 2 minutes

Serving: 2

Ingredients:

2 bananas, peeled

1 cup plain or vanilla yogurt

1 1/2 tablespoons honey

1/2 teaspoon fresh ginger, grated

Instructions:

1. Place the bananas, yogurt, honey, and ginger in the medium or large Magic Bullet blending cup. Screw on the blade assembly and place the cup on the Magic Bullet. Press down to blend.

2. When the Magic Bullet is finished blending, pour the smoothie into two glasses and enjoy.

Nutritional Info: Calories: 242, Sodium: 88 mg, Dietary Fiber: 3.2 g, Fat: 1.9 g, Carbs: 48.9 g, Protein: 8.4 g.

Orange Creamsicle Smoothie

Perfect for a hit summer day, after a workout, or just for a healthy and delicious dessert smoothie. This fun take on an ice cream truck classic is cure to please.

Prep time: 2 minutes
Cook time: 2 minutes
Servings: 2

Ingredients:

2 large oranges, peeled and seeds removed

1/2 cup vanilla yogurt

4 tablespoons frozen orange concentrate

8 ice cubes

Instructions:

1. Place the oranges, yogurt, juice concentrate, and ice cubes in the large Magic Bullet blending cup. Screw on the blade assembly and place the cup on the Magic Bullet. Press down to blend.

2. When the Magic Bullet is finished blending, pour the smoothie into two glasses and enjoy.

Nutritional Info: Calories: 141, Sodium: 44 mg, Dietary Fiber: 4.6 g, Fat: 1 g, Carbs: 28.6 g, Protein: 5.5 g.

Strawberry Orange Smoothie

This refreshing smooth is great because it packs a whole day's worth of vitamin C into one delicious drink that you can take with you on the go thanks to the Magic Bullet's handy spout top lids.

Prep time: 2 minutes

Cook time: 2 minutes

Servings: 2

Ingredients:

1 cup frozen strawberries

2 bananas

1 large orange, peeled and seeds removed

1/2 cup orange juice

Instructions:

1. Place the strawberries, bananas, oranges, and orange juice into the Medium Magic Bullet blending cup. Screw on the blade assembly and place the cup on the Magic Bullet. Press down to blend.

2. When the Magic Bullet is finished blending, pour the smoothie into two glasses and enjoy.

Nutritional Info: Calories: 201, Sodium: 2 mg, Dietary Fiber: 6.9 g, Fat: 0.6 g, Carbs: 50.7 g, Protein: 2.6 g.

Pina Colada Smoothie

This fun island cocktail inspired smoothie is alcohol free and a great healthy way to start the day, or for relaxing after work.

Prep time: 2 minutes
Cook time: 2 minutes
Servings: 2

Ingredients:

1 cup frozen pineapple chunks

1 cup fresh coconut flesh

1 cup plain or vanilla yogurt

8 ice cubes

Instructions:

1. Place the pineapple, coconut, yogurt, and ice cubes in the Medium Magic Bullet blending cup. Screw on the blade assembly and place the cup on the Magic Bullet. Press down to blend.

2. When the Magic Bullet is finished blending, pour the smoothie into two glasses and enjoy.

Nutritional Info: Calories: 334, Sodium: 96 mg, Dietary Fiber: 5 g, Fat: 15 g, Carbs: 41.9 g, Protein: 8.8 g.

Kiwi Strawberry Smoothie

Full of vitamin C and fiber, this delicious sweet smoothie is great after a workout or on a hot summer day. For an even more robust flavor try using fresh strawberries instead of frozen.

Prep time: 2 minutes
Cook time: 2 minutes
Servings: 2

Ingredients:

2 kiwis, peeled and sliced

1 cup frozen strawberries

1 banana, peeled

1 1/2 cups apple juice

Instructions:

1. Place the kiwis, strawberries, banana, and apple juice in the 18 or Medium Magic Bullet blending cup. Screw on the blade assembly and place the cup on the Magic Bullet. Press down to blend.

2. When the Magic Bullet is finished blending, pour the smoothie into two glasses and enjoy.

Nutritional Info: Calories: 209, Sodium: 10 mg, Dietary Fiber: 5.7 g, Fat: 0.8 g, Carbs: 52.1 g, Protein: 1.7 g.

Cantaloupe Smoothie

Delicious and subtle melon blends perfectly with tangy citrus to create a smoothie that is truly refreshing and healthy. You can try substituting cantaloupe with other melons for different flavors.

Prep time: 2 minutes

Cook time: 2 minutes

Servings: 2

Ingredients:

2 cups fresh cantaloupe chunks

juice of 1/2 lime

2 tablespoons honey

1/4 cup apple juice

1/4 cup water

1 cup ice cubes

Instructions:

1. Place the cantaloupe, lime juice, honey, apple juice, water, and ice cubes in the large Magic Bullet blending cup. Screw on the blade assembly and place the cup on the Magic Bullet. Press down to blend.

2. When the Magic Bullet is finished blending, pour the smoothie into two glasses and enjoy.

Nutritional Info: Calories: 134, Sodium: 28 mg, Dietary Fiber: 1.6 g, Fat: 0.4 g, Carbs: 34.5 g, Protein: 1.4 g.

Apple Carrot Smoothie

This easy to make nutritious smoothie is a perfect way to get the kids to eat their carrots. It's also a refreshing drink for a hot summer day.

Prep time: 5 minutes

Cook time: 2 minutes

Servings: 2

Ingredients:

2 carrots, peeled and chopped

1 large apple, peeled and chopped

1 cup apple juice

1 cup carrot juice

1 1/2 cups ice

Instructions:

1. Place the carrots, apples, apple juice, carrot juice, and ice in the large Magic Bullet blending cup. Screw on the blade assembly and place the cup on the Magic Bullet. Press down to blend.

2. When the Magic Bullet is finished blending, pour the smoothie into two glasses and enjoy.

Nutritional Info: Calories: 187, Sodium: 88 mg, Dietary Fiber: 5.4 g, Fat: 0.5 g, Carbs: 46.4 g, Protein: 2 g.

Cherry Vanilla Smoothie

This rich and delicious smoothie tastes like dessert but it's actually healthy and provides a punch of antioxidants and vitamins.

Prep time: 5 minutes

Cook time: 2 minutes

Servings: 2

Ingredients:

1 1/2 cups whole milk

1 1/2 cups frozen cherries, pitted

2 tablespoons honey

1/2 teaspoon vanilla extract

1/4 teaspoon almond extract

1/4 cup ice cubes

Instructions:

1. Place the milk, cherries, honey, vanilla extract, almond extract, and ice cubes into the large Magic Bullet blending cup. Screw on the blade assembly and place the cup on the Magic Bullet. Press down to blend.

2. When the Magic Bullet is finished blending, pour the smoothie into two glasses and enjoy.

Nutritional Info: Calories: 230, Sodium: 76 mg, Dietary Fiber: 1.9 g, Fat: 0.5 g, Carbs: 6.5 g, Protein: 7 g.

Mango Acai Berry Smoothie

This healthy smoothie uses acai berries which are famous for their antioxidant powers. Combined with the sweet tangy flavor of mango, this is a smoothie you will want to make every day.

Prep time: 5 minutes

Cook time: 2 minutes

Servings: 2

Ingredients:

1/2 cup acai berries

1 large mango, chopped into chunks

1/2 cup orange juice

1 cup ice

Instructions:

1. Place the acai berries, mango, orange juice, and ice into the medium or large Magic Bullet blending cup. Screw on the blade assembly and place the cup on the Magic Bullet. Press down to blend.

2. When the Magic Bullet is finished blending, pour the smoothie into two glasses and enjoy. Or take your smoothie on the go with the Magic Bullet's spout top cup.

Nutritional Info: Calories: 146, Sodium: 8 mg, Dietary Fiber: 3.6 g, Fat: 2 g, Carbs: 32.6 g, Protein: 1.8 g.

Kale and Cucumber Smoothie

This hydrating smoothie is packed with nutrients thanks to hearty kale leaves and delicate cucumber. The addition of citrus, adds just a hint of brightness.

Prep time: 5 minutes
Cook time: 2 minutes
Servings: 2

Ingredients:

1 cup kale, chopped

1 cucumber, chopped

1/4 cup orange juice

1/4 cup apple juice

1/4 cup lime juice

Instructions:

1. Chop the kale and cucumber and place in the medium or large Magic Bullet blending cup with the orange, apple, and lime juice. Screw on the blade assembly and place the cup on the Magic Bullet. Press down to blend.

2. When the Magic Bullet is finished blending, pour the smoothie into two glasses and enjoy.

Nutritional Info: Calories: 69, Sodium: 19 mg, Dietary Fiber: 1.4 g, Fat: 0.3 g, Carbs: 16.1 g, Protein: 2.2 g.

Spinach Citrus Smoothie

This vegetable and citrus smoothie packs an entire day's worth of iron, vitamin C and Vitamin D. And best of all, it's a delicious and easy way to eat your vegetables.

Prep time: 5 minutes

Cook time: 2 minutes

Servings: 2

Ingredients:

2 cups fresh spinach

1 large orange, peeled and seeds removed

1/2 cup blueberries

Juice from 1/2 lemon

1 tablespoon honey or agave syrup

Instructions:

1. Chop the spinach and place in a medium or large Magic Bullet blending cup with the orange, blueberries, lemon juice, and honey. Screw on the blade assembly and place the cup on the Magic Bullet. Press down to blend.

2. When the Magic Bullet is finished blending, pour the smoothie into two glasses and enjoy.

Nutritional Info: Calories: 106, Sodium: 25 mg, Dietary Fiber: 3.8 g, Fat: 0.4 g, Carbs: 26.9 g, Protein: 2.1 g.

Raspberry Coconut Smoothie

The flavors of sweet fresh raspberries and earthy coconut pair perfectly for a smoothie high in vitamins and fiber. This smoothie is the perfect way to start your day.

Prep time: 5 minutes
Cook time: 2 minutes
Servings: 2

Ingredients:

1/2 cup fresh raspberries

1 cup unsweetened coconut milk

1 banana, peeled

1/4 cup coconut flakes

1 tablespoon honey

Instructions:

1. Place the raspberries, coconut milk, banana, coconut flakes, and honey in the small or Medium Magic Bullet blending cup. Screw on the blade assembly and place the cup on the Magic Bullet. Press down to blend.

2. When the Magic Bullet is finished blending, pour the smoothie into two glasses and enjoy, or take on the go with the Magic Bullet spout top cups.

Nutritional Info: Calories: 412, Sodium: 21 mg, Dietary Fiber: 7.1 g, Fat: 32.3 g, Carbs: 34 g, Protein: 4.1 g.

Sweet Chia Smoothie

Chia seeds are all the rage right now because they are loaded with huge nutrition in a small package. The combination of earthy chia seeds and tropical fruits makes this smoothie a hit every time.

Prep time: 5 minutes
Cook time: 2 minutes
Servings: 2

Ingredients:

2 tablespoons chia seeds

1 cup frozen mango chunks

1 cup frozen pineapple chunks

1 cup almond milk

1 tablespoon honey or agave syrup

Instructions:

1. Place the chia seeds, mango chunks, pineapple chunks, almond milk, and honey into the medium or large Magic Bullet blending cup. Screw on the blade assembly and place the cup on the Magic Bullet. Press down to blend.

2. When the Magic Bullet is finished blending, pour the smoothie into two glasses and enjoy, or take on the go with the Magic Bullet spout top cups.

Nutritional Info: Calories: 523, Sodium: 22 mg, Dietary Fiber: 10.3 g, Fat: 32 g, Carbs: 59.9 g, Protein: 7 g.

Super Green Smoothie

This smoothie is perfect if you want to pack all of your daily vegetables into one delicious serving. A great way to start the day.

Prep time: 2 minutes

Cook time: 2 minutes

Servings: 2

Ingredients:

1 cup fresh spinach

1/2 cup kale, chopped

1/2 cucumber, chopped

1 banana, peeled

1/2 pear, chopped

1/2 cup orange juice

1 cup almond milk

Instructions:

1. Place the spinach, kale, cucumber, banana, pear, orange juice, and almond milk into the large Magic Bullet blending cup. Screw on the blade assembly and place the cup on the Magic Bullet. Press down to blend.

2. When the Magic Bullet is finished blending, pour the smoothie into two glasses and enjoy, or take on the go with the Magic Bullet spout top cups.

Nutritional Info: Calories: 400, Sodium: 40 mg, Dietary Fiber: 6.3 g, Fat: 29.1 g, Carbs: 36.9 g, Protein: 5.4 g.

Pomegranate Berry Smoothie

Pomegranates are known for their nutritional powers and this robust flavored smoothie is the perfect jolt you need to get your day started. You might not even need that cup of coffee.

Prep time: 2 minutes

Cook time: 2 minutes

Servings: 2

Ingredients:

1 cup pomegranate juice

1 cup plain or vanilla yogurt

1 cup frozen strawberries

1/2 cup frozen blueberries

1/2 cup frozen blackberries or raspberries

Instructions:

1. Place the pomegranate juice, yogurt, strawberries, blueberries, and blackberries in the medium or large Magic Bullet blending cup. Screw on the blade assembly and place the cup on the Magic Bullet. Press down to blend.

2. When the Magic Bullet is finished blending, pour the smoothie into two glasses and enjoy, or take on the go with the Magic Bullet spout top cups.

Nutritional Info: Calories: 223, Sodium: 91 mg, Dietary Fiber: 4.3 g, Fat: 1.8 g, Carbs: 42.3 g, Protein: 7.8 g.

Honeydew Mint Smoothie

This light and refreshing smoothie uses the mild flavors of honeydew, mint, and fresh pears to create a beverage that is perfect for relaxing on a warm summer day.

Prep time: 5 minutes

Cook time: 2 minutes

Servings: 2

Ingredients:

2 cups honeydew melon, chopped

2 pears, chopped

1/2 cup apple juice

1 cup ice cubes

1/2 cup fresh peppermint leaves

Instructions:

1. Place the melon, pears, apple juice, ice, and mint leaves into the medium-large Magic Bullet blending cup. Screw on the blade assembly and place the cup on the Magic Bullet. Press down to blend.

2. When the Magic Bullet is finished blending, pour the smoothie into two glasses and enjoy, or take on the go with the Magic Bullet spout top cups.

Nutritional Info: Calories: 220, Sodium: 46 mg, Dietary Fiber: 9.5 g, Fat: 0.8 g, Carbs: 56.2 g, Protein: 2.5 g.

Green Tea Smoothie

Green tea has many nutritional values including valuable antioxidants. This green tea smoothie is packed with nutrition and fun tropical flavors.

Prep time: 2 minutes
Cook time: 2 minutes
Servings: 2

Ingredients:

1/2 cup cold green tea

1 cup fresh pineapple, chopped

2 kiwi, peeled and chopped

2 bananas, peeled

1/3 cup ice cubes

Instructions:

1. Place the green tea, pineapple, kiwi, banana, and ice cubes into the medium or large Magic Bullet blending cup. Screw on the blade assembly and place the cup on the Magic Bullet. Press down to blend.

2. When the Magic Bullet is finished blending, pour the smoothie into two glasses and enjoy, or take on the go with the Magic Bullet spout top cups.

Nutritional Info: Calories: 212, Sodium: 4 mg, Dietary Fiber: 6.5 g, Fat: 0.9 g, Carbs: 53.5 g, Protein: 2.6 g.

Peanut Butter Banana Smoothie

This rich and flavorful smoothie uses peanut butter for a thick and delicious flavor that the kids will love.

Prep time: 5 minutes
Cook time: 2 minutes
Servings: 2

Ingredients:

2 bananas, peeled

1 cup whole milk

2 tablespoons peanut butter

1 cup ice cubes

Instructions:

1. Place the bananas, milk, peanut butter, and ice cubes into the large Magic Bullet blending cup. Screw on the blade assembly and place the cup on the Magic Bullet. Press down to blend.

2. When the Magic Bullet is finished blending, pour the smoothie into two glasses and enjoy, or take on the go with the Magic Bullet spout top cups.

Nutritional Info: Calories: 273, Sodium: 123 mg, Dietary Fiber: 4 g, Fat: 12.4 g, Carbs: 35.6 g, Protein: 9.2 g.

6

MILKSHAKES

"The Five Dollar Shake"

This classic vanilla shake is a perfectly balanced soda fountain favorite with the perfect texture and flavor. Not too sweet and not too thick. It's a darn good shake.

Prep time: 5 minutes

Cook time: 1 minute

Servings: 2

Ingredients:

1 pint good quality vanilla ice cream

1/4 cup whole milk

1 teaspoon vanilla extract

1/4 teaspoon kosher salt

Instructions:

1. Place the ice cream, milk, vanilla, and salt into the large Magic Bullet blending cup. Screw on the blade assembly and place the cup on the Magic Bullet. Press down to blend until smooth, about five seconds.

2. When the Magic Bullet is finished blending, pour the shake into two glasses, top with a cherry, and enjoy.

Nutritional Info: Calories: 93, Sodium: 330 mg, Dietary Fiber: 0.3 g, Fat: 4.5 g, Carbs: 9.7 g, Protein: 2.1 g.

Mixed Berry Shake

This shake is the perfect cross between a milkshake and a smoothie. Perfect for a hot summer day or a quick and easy dessert.

Prep time: 5 minutes
Cook time: 2 minutes
Servings: 2

Ingredients:

1 pint strawberry ice cream

1/4 cup whole milk

1/2 cup fresh or frozen raspberries

1/2 cup fresh or frozen blueberries

Instructions:

1. Place the ice cream, milk, and berries into the large Magic Bullet blending cup. Screw on the blade assembly and place the cup on the Magic Bullet. Press down to blend until smooth, about ten seconds.

2. When the Magic Bullet is finished blending, pour the shake into two glasses, and enjoy.

Nutritional Info: Calories: 172, Sodium: 40 mg, Dietary Fiber: 3.9 g, Fat: 4.7 g, Carbs: 31 g, Protein: 2.9 g.

Chocolate and Banana Shake

This easy to make shake is a fun twist on the classic chocolate shake, and is packed with plenty or rich chocolate flavor. It's also a great way to make use of bananas that are a little past their prime.

Prep time: 5 minutes
Cook time: 2 minutes
Servings: 2

Ingredients:

1 pint chocolate ice cream

2 bananas, chopped into rounds and frozen

1/4 cup whole milk

3 tablespoons chocolate syrup

Instructions:

1. In a small glass, mix the milk and chocolate syrup. Place the ice cream, banana chunks, and chocolate milk into the large Magic Bullet blending cup. Screw on the blade assembly and place the cup on the Magic Bullet. Press down to blend until smooth, about ten seconds.

2. When the Magic Bullet is finished blending, pour the shake into two glasses, and enjoy.

Nutritional Info: Calories: 270, Sodium: 60 mg, Dietary Fiber: 4.1 g, Fat: 4.7 g, Carbs: 5.2 g, Protein: 4 g.

Key Lime Shake

This delightful milkshake is like drinking a key lime pie whenever you want. Tangy key lime juice and rich vanilla ice cream pair perfectly for a treat the whole family will love.

Prep time: 2 minutes

Cook time: 2 minutes

Servings: 2

Ingredients:

1 pint vanilla ice cream

1/2 cup whole milk

Juice and zest from 6 key limes

Instructions:

1. Place the ice cream, milk, and lime juice and half of the zest into the large Magic Bullet blending cup. Screw on the blade assembly and place the cup on the Magic Bullet. Press down to blend until smooth, about five seconds.

2. When the Magic Bullet is finished blending, pour the shake into two glasses, top with remaining zest, and enjoy.

Nutritional Info: Calories: 240, Sodium: 55 mg, Dietary Fiber: 11.9 g, Fat: 5.9 g, Carbs: 59 g, Protein: 7.5 g.

Cookies and Cream Shake

This fun shake combines chocolate cookies and rich vanilla ice cream for a treat that is perfect for entertaining or a special dessert.

Prep time: 10 minutes

Cook time: 2 minutes

Servings: 2

Ingredients:

1 pint vanilla ice cream

1 cup chocolate wafer cookies

1/4 cup milk

Instructions:

1. In a small bowl, pour the milk over the chocolate cookies and allow them to sit until the cookies become soft, about 10 minutes.

2. When the cookies are soft, pour them with the milk into the large Magic Bullet blending cup with the ice cream. Screw on the blade assembly and place the cup on the Magic Bullet. Press down to blend until smooth, about five seconds.

3. When the Magic Bullet is finished blending, pour the shake into two glasses, and enjoy.

Nutritional Info: Calories: 326, Sodium: 366 mg, Dietary Fiber: 2.2 g, Fat: 12.1 g, Carbs: 50 g, Protein: 5.9 g.

Chocolate and Peanut Butter Shake

Is there a better combination than chocolate and peanut butter? Nope. This shake perfectly balances rich chocolate ice cream and creamy peanut butter for a treat that will be a hit with friends and family.

Prep time: 2 minutes

Cook time: 2 minutes

Servings: 2

Ingredients:

1 pint chocolate ice cream

1/2 cup whole milk

1/2 cup creamy peanut butter

Instructions:

1. Place the ice cream, milk, and peanut butter in the large Magic Bullet blending cup. Screw on the blade assembly and place the cup on the Magic Bullet. Press down to blend until smooth, about five seconds.

2. When the Magic Bullet is finished blending, pour the shake into two glasses, and enjoy.

Nutritional Info: Calories: 484, Sodium: 347 mg, Dietary Fiber: 4.1 g, Fat: 37.9 g, Carbs: 23.5 g, Protein: 19.2 g.

Salted Caramel Shake

Salted caramel is amazing because it is the perfect blend of salty and sweet. This delicious shake is rich and decadent, and sure to be a hit with the whole family.

Prep time: 2 minutes

Cook time: 2 minutes

Servings: 2

Ingredients:

1 pint vanilla ice cream

1/4 cup whole milk

3 tablespoons caramel sauce

1/2 teaspoon kosher salt

2 tablespoons crushed pretzels

Instructions:

1. lace the ice cream, milk, 1 tablespoon of caramel sauce, and salt into the large Magic Bullet blending cup. Screw on the blade assembly and place the cup on the Magic Bullet. Press down to blend until smooth, about five seconds.

2. Drizzle the remaining caramel sauce into the inside of two tall glasses.

3. When the Magic Bullet is finished blending, pour the shake into two glasses, top with the crushed pretzels, and enjoy.

Nutritional Info: Calories: 269, Sodium: 167 mg, Dietary Fiber: 1.5 g, Fat: 5 g, Carbs: 51.6 g, Protein: 5.6 g.

Mocha Coffee Chip Shake

This delightful combination of coffee and chocolate is rich and satisfying and makes for an easy dessert after a long day.

Prep time: 5 minutes

Cook time: 2 minutes

Servings: 2

Ingredients:

1/2 pint chocolate ice cream

1/2 pint coffee ice cream

1/4 whole milk

1/4 cup chocolate syrup

1/4 semi sweet chocolate chips

Instructions:

1. Place the ice cream, milk, and chocolate chips in the large Magic Bullet blending cup. Screw on the blade assembly and place the cup on the Magic Bullet. Press down to blend about five seconds until the chips have broken down a bit.

2. Drizzle the chocolate sauce into the inside of two tall glasses.

3. Pour the shake into two glasses and enjoy.

Nutritional Info: Calories: 477, Sodium: 132 mg, Dietary Fiber: 1.1 g, Fat: 19.2 g, Carbs: 64.8 g, Protein: 8.9 g.

Malted Shake

This old fashioned shake was once one of the most popular shakes at soda fountains across the country. It may not be as popular as it once was, but once you try it you will want to make it all the time.

Prep time: 2 minutes

Cook time: 2 minutes

Servings: 2

Ingredients:

1 pint vanilla or coffee ice cream

1/2 cup whole milk

4 tablespoons malted milk powder

1/2 teaspoon vanilla extract

Instructions:

1. Place the ice cream, milk, malted milk powder, and vanilla extract into the large Magic Bullet blending cup. Screw on the blade assembly and place the cup on the Magic Bullet. Press down to blend until smooth, about ten seconds.

2. When the Magic Bullet is finished blending, pour the shake into two glasses, and enjoy.

Nutritional Info: Calories: 632, Sodium: 56 mg, Dietary Fiber: 0 g, Fat: 2.7 g, Carbs: 30 g, Protein: 2.7 g.

7

COCKTAILS

Classic Margarita

This Mexican cocktail is a favorite all over the world these days thanks to its tangy and fun flavors. You can use your Magic Bullet to make perfectly blended margaritas that will impress your guests.

Prep time: 5 minutes

Cook time: 2 minutes

Servings: 2

Ingredients:

6 ounces tequila

4 ounces fresh lime juice

2 ounces simple syrup

2 teaspoons triple sec

2 cups ice cubes

Kosher salt (optional)

Instructions:

1. Place the tequila, lime juice, simple syrup, triple sec, and ice cubes in the large Magic Bullet blending cup. Screw on the blade assembly and place the cup on the Magic Bullet. Press down to blend until smooth, about ten seconds.

2. Wet the rims of two glasses and press into the kosher salt.

3. When the Magic Bullet is finished blending, pour the shake into two glasses, and enjoy.

Nutritional Info: Calories: 332, Sodium: 412 mg, Dietary Fiber: 0.3 g, Fat: 0 g, Carbs: 28.7 g, Protein: 0.2 g.

Berry Rum Cocktail

This refreshing cocktail is perfect for entertaining at a party on a hot summer day. Your guest will want to know how they can make such a fun and inventive cocktail.

Prep time: 5 minutes
Cook time: 2 minutes
Servings: 4

Ingredients:

1 cup frozen raspberries

1 cup frozen blackberries

1 cup frozen blueberries

8 ounces light rum

4 ounces simple syrup

2 ounces fresh lime juice

2 cups ice cubes

Instructions:

1. In the large Magic Bullet blending cup, combine the berries, rum, simple syrup, lime juice, and ice cubes. Screw on the blade assembly and place the cup on the Magic Bullet. Press down to blend until smooth, about ten seconds.

2. When the Magic Bullet is finished blending, pour the shake into four glasses, and enjoy.

Nutritional Info: Calories: 326, Sodium: 22 mg, Dietary Fiber: 5.6 g, Fat: 0.4 g, Carbs: 50 g, Protein: 1.3 g.

Classic Pina Colada

This tropical classic has been a vacation favorite for many decades, but thanks to your Magic Bullet you can make delicious piña coladas whenever you want. Perfectly flavored and perfectly blended.

Prep time: 5 minutes

Cook time: 2 minutes

Servings: 2

Ingredients:

3 ounces coconut cream

3 ounces pineapple juice

3 ounces golden rum

1 cup ice cubes

Instructions:

1. Place the coconut cream, pineapple juice, rum, and ice cubes in the large Magic Bullet blending cup. Screw on the blade assembly and place the cup on the Magic Bullet. Press down to blend until smooth, about ten seconds.

2. When the Magic Bullet is finished blending, pour the shake into two glasses, and enjoy.

Nutritional Info: Calories: 219, Sodium: 8 mg, Dietary Fiber: 1 g, Fat: 10.2 g, Carbs: 7.8 g, Protein: 1.1 g.

Strawberry Lime Daiquiri

This tangy take on the classic strawberry daiquiri is a bold and refreshing cocktail that is perfect for summer celebrations or just relaxing after a day at the beach. Your Magic Bullet guarantees perfectly blended daiquiris whenever you want.

Prep time: 2 minutes

Cook time: 2 minutes

Servings: 2

Ingredients:

10 fresh strawberries

4 ounces light rum

2 ounces fresh lime juice

1 ounce triple sec

1 ounce simple syrup

2 cups ice cubes

Instructions:

1. Place the strawberries, rum, lime juice, triple sec, simple syrup, and ice into the large Magic Bullet blending cup. Screw on the blade assembly and place the cup on the Magic Bullet. Press down to blend until smooth, about ten seconds.

2. When the Magic Bullet is finished blending, pour the shake into two glasses, and enjoy.

Nutritional Info: Calories: 245, Sodium: 1117 mg, Dietary Fiber: 1.3 g, Fat: 0.2 g, Carbs: 18.9 g, Protein: 0.5 g.

The Blue Hawaiian

This classic 1950s cocktail took off when Hawaiian vacations and Tiki bars were all the rage. It continues to be a blended favorite because of it's fun flavor and unmistakable color.

Prep time: 2 minutes

Cook time: 2 minutes

Servings: 2

Ingredients:

2 ounces light rum

2 ounces blue Curacao

4 ounces pineapple juice

2 ounces coconut cream

2 cups ice cubes

2 cherries (for garnish)

Instructions:

1. Place the rum, blue Curacao, pineapple juice, coconut cream, and ice in the large Magic Bullet blending cup. Screw on the blade assembly and place the cup on the Magic Bullet. Press down to blend until smooth, about ten seconds.

2. When the Magic Bullet is finished blending, pour the shake into two glasses, and enjoy.

Nutritional Info: Calories: 199, Sodium: 13 mg, Dietary Fiber: 0.7 g, Fat: 6.8 g, Carbs: 17.9 g, Protein: 0.9 g.

Mudslide

This fun drink works as a cocktail or a boozy dessert that is sure to be a hit at parties. The Magic Bullets powerful blades and motor ensure your mudslides are perfectly smooth and creamy every time.

Prep time: 2 minutes
Cook time: 2 minutes
Servings: 4

Ingredients:

4 ounces vodka

4 ounces Kahlua

4 ounces Irish cream liqueur

3 tablespoons chocolate syrup

4 cups ice cubes

1/2 cup whipped cream

Instructions:

1. Place the vodka, Kahlua, Irish cream liqueur, chocolate syrup, and ice cubes into the large Magic Bullet blending cup. Screw on the blade assembly and place the cup on the Magic Bullet. Press down to blend until smooth, about ten seconds.

2. When the Magic Bullet is finished blending, pour the shake into four glasses, and top with whipped cream to serve.

Nutritional Info: Calories: 563, Sodium: 105 mg, Dietary Fiber: 0.4 g, Fat: 17.9 g, Carbs: 47.3 g, Protein: 3.7 g.

Kiwi Margarita

This fun take on the classic margarita combines the tangy flavors of kiwi and lime for an intense burst of flavor that is sure to delight your guests. This cocktail can be enjoyed blended or on the rocks.

Prep time: 2 minutes

Cook time: 2 minutes

Servings: 4

Ingredients:

8 ounces gold tequila

4 ounces triple sec

2 kiwis, peeled

8 ounces fresh lime juice

2 cups ice cubes

Instructions:

1. Place the tequila, triple sec, kiwis, lime juice, and ice in the large Magic Bullet blending cup. Screw on the blade assembly and place the cup on the Magic Bullet. Press down to blend until smooth, about ten seconds.

2. When the Magic Bullet is finished blending, pour the shake into four glasses, and enjoy.

Nutritional Info: Calories: 264, Sodium: 2214 mg, Dietary Fiber: 1.4 g, Fat: 0.2 g, Carbs: 10.4 g, Protein: 0.7 g.

Frozen Greyhound

This blended version of the classic Greyhound cocktail is a refreshing and tart. The perfect accompaniment to tapas or brick oven pizza.

Prep time: 2 minutes
Cook time: 2 minutes
Servings: 2

Ingredients:

1 cup fresh grapefruit juice

4 ounces vodka

1 ounce simple syrup

1 cup ice cubes

Instructions:

1. Place the grapefruit juice, vodka, simple syrup, and ice into the large Magic Bullet blending cup. Screw on the blade assembly and place the cup on the Magic Bullet. Press down to blend until smooth, about ten seconds.

2. When the Magic Bullet is finished blending, pour the shake into two glasses, and enjoy.

Nutritional Info: Calories: 213, Sodium: 11 mg, Dietary Fiber: 1.3 g, Fat: 0.1 g, Carbs: 21.2 g, Protein: 0.7 g.

Blended Russian

The Dude would abide this blended and creamy take on the classic White Russian. Your Magic Bullet guarantees your blended drinks always come out smooth and delicious.

Prep time: 2 minutes

Cook time: 2 minutes

Servings: 2

Ingredients:

1/2 cup whole milk or half and half

4 ounces vodka

2 ounces Kahlua

1 cup ice cubes

Instructions:

1. Place the milk, vodka, Kahlua, and ice cubes in the medium or large Magic Bullet blending cup. Screw on the blade assembly and place the cup on the Magic Bullet. Press down to blend until smooth, about ten seconds.

2. When the Magic Bullet is finished blending, pour the shake into two glasses, and enjoy.

Nutritional Info: Calories: 255, Sodium: 27 mg, Dietary Fiber: 0 g, Fat: 2.1 g, Carbs: 11.9 g, Protein: 2 g.

Classic Banana Daiquiri

This classic Cuban cocktail is the perfect way to cool down on a hit summer day in the Islands. Fresh banana means authentic flavors and smooth texture with just the right amount of sweetness.

Prep time: 5 minutes

Cook time: 2 minutes

Servings: 2

Ingredients:

1 large banana, peeled and sliced

4 ounces light rum

1 ounce triple sec

2 ounces fresh lime juice

1 ounce simple syrup

1 cup ice cubes

Instructions:

1. Place the banana, rum, triple sec, lime juice, simple syrup, and ice into the large Magic Bullet blending cup. Screw on the blade assembly and place the cup on the Magic Bullet. Press down to blend until smooth, about ten seconds.

2. When the Magic Bullet is finished blending, pour the shake into two glasses, and enjoy.

Nutritional Info: Calories: 286, Sodium: 1117 mg, Dietary Fiber: 1.9 g, Fat: 0.2 g, Carbs: 29.8 g, Protein: 0.9 g.

8

PROTEIN SHAKES

Super Vanilla Espresso Shake

This protein-rich shake is the perfect treat after a big workout, but it's so delicious you might find yourself blending up a batch as a fun alternative to dessert.

Prep time: 2 minutes

Cook time: 2 minutes

Servings: 1

Ingredients:

1 1/2 cups almond milk

6 tablespoons vanilla protein powder

1 shot espresso

1/2 cup coffee ice cream

Instructions:

1. Place the almond milk, protein powder, espresso, and ice cream into the Medium Magic Bullet blending cup. Screw on the blade assembly and place the cup on the Magic Bullet. Press down to blend until smooth, about five seconds.

2. When the Magic Bullet is finished blending, pour the shake into a glass, and enjoy.

Nutritional Info: Calories: 995, Sodium: 157 mg, Dietary Fiber: 9.9 g, Fat: 91.4 g, Carbs: 35.4 g, Protein: 22.9 g.

Cinnamon Protein Shake

This rich and creamy protein shakes is delicious and full of muscle building protein for a shake that can take the place of a meal. Your Magic Bullet's powerful blending motor means your shakes are smooth and creamy in no time.

Prep time: 2 minutes

Cook time: 2 minutes

Servings: 1

Ingredients:

6 tablespoons vanilla protein powder

1/4 teaspoon cinnamon

1/4 teaspoon vanilla extract

1 cup almond milk

1 tablespoon vanilla pudding mix

1 cup ice

Instructions:

1. Place the protein powder, cinnamon, vanilla, milk, pudding mix, and ice into the Medium Magic Bullet blending cup. Screw on the blade assembly and place the cup on the Magic Bullet. Press down to blend until smooth, about five seconds.

2. When the Magic Bullet is finished blending, pour the shake into a glass, and enjoy.

Nutritional Info: Calories: 733, Sodium: 278 mg, Dietary Fiber: 7.5 g, Fat: 59.4 g, Carbs: 40.9 g, Protein: 19.9 g.

Supercharged Banana Shake

This rich and creamy banana shake is fortified with nutritious almonds and protein powder for a shake that packs as much nutrition as possible into a single beverage.

Prep time: 2 minutes

Cook time: 2 minutes

Servings: 1

Ingredients:

1 large banana, peeled

1/2 cup almond milk

6 tablespoons vanilla protein powder

12 almonds

1/2 cup ice cubes

Instructions:

1. Place the banana, almond milk, protein powder, almonds, and ice into the Medium Magic Bullet blending cup. Screw on the blade assembly and place the cup on the Magic Bullet. Press down to blend until smooth, about ten seconds or until all of the almonds have been pureed.

2. When the Magic Bullet is finished blending, pour the shake into a glass, and enjoy.

Nutritional Info: Calories: 574, Sodium: 96 mg, Dietary Fiber: 9.7 g, Fat: 38.3 g, Carbs: 47.2 g, Protein: 20.7 g.

Berry Power Shake

This protein shake is packed with muscle building protein, but it also has a full day's worth of vitamin C as well as a full complement of other vitamins and minerals. This shake is the perfect way to start out your day. Everyday.

Prep time: 2 minutes
Cook time: 2 minutes
Servings: 2

Ingredients:

1/2 cup fresh or frozen raspberries

1/2 cup fresh or frozen strawberries

1/2 cup fresh or frozen blueberries

1/2 cup fresh or frozen cherries

1/2 cup fresh or frozen blackberries

12 tablespoons protein powder

1 cup almond milk

Instructions:

1. Place the raspberries, strawberries, blueberries, cherries, blackberries, protein powder, and milk into the large Magic Bullet blending cup. Screw on the blade assembly and place the cup on the Magic Bullet. Press down to blend until smooth, about five seconds.

2. When the Magic Bullet is finished blending, pour the shake into two glasses, and enjoy.

Nutritional Info: Calories: 527, Sodium: 284 mg, Dietary Fiber: 9.6 g, Fat: 29.2 g, Carbs: 39.2 g, Protein: 34.3 g.

Strawberry Banana Protein Shake

This simple shake is the perfect way to load up on vital protein after a big workout or a long run. It's important to eat protein as quickly as possible after exercise for proper muscle repair. Luckily, your Magic Bullet makes perfect protein shakes in no time.

Prep time: 2 minutes

Cook time: 2 minutes

Servings: 2

Ingredients:

2 bananas, peeled

1 1/2 cups frozen strawberries

1/2 cup plain greek yogurt

12 tablespoons protein powder

Instructions:

1. Place the banana, strawberries, yogurt, and protein powder into the large Magic Bullet blending cup. Screw on the blade assembly and place the cup on the Magic Bullet. Press down to blend until smooth, about five seconds.

2. When the Magic Bullet is finished blending, pour the shake into two glasses, and enjoy.

Nutritional Info: Calories: 287, Sodium: 283 mg, Dietary Fiber: 5.3 g, Fat: 0.4 g, Carbs: 38 g, Protein: 35.8 g.

Peanut Butter and Jelly Protein Shake

Chances are the famous sandwich this shake is based on was a big part of your childhood. Relive your childhood memories and get a big dose of protein with this delicious shake.

Prep time: 2 minutes
Cook time: 2 minutes
Servings: 2

Ingredients:

1 cup frozen strawberries

1 cup frozen raspberries

4 tablespoons creamy peanut butter

1/4 cup protein powder

1 cup almond milk

Instructions:

1. Place the strawberries, raspberries, peanut butter, protein powder, and milk into the large Magic Bullet blending cup. Screw on the blade assembly and place the cup on the Magic Bullet. Press down to blend until smooth, about five seconds.

2. When the Magic Bullet is finished blending, pour the shake into two glasses, and enjoy.

Nutritional Info: Calories: 658, Sodium: 254 mg, Dietary Fiber: 11.6 g, Fat: 44.9 g, Carbs: 52.2 g, Protein: 21.6 g.

Green Flaxseed Protein Shake

This super shake is packed with a huge dose of concentrated nutrition. Who knew it was so easy to get a whole day's worth of fruits and vegetables in one easy shake.

Prep time: 2 minutes
Cook time: 2 minutes
Servings: 1

Ingredients:

1 cup baby spinach

1 cup baby kale

1/4 cup frozen mango

1/4 cup frozen strawberries

1/2 banana

1 tablespoon ground flaxseed

1 tablespoon ground chia seeds

6 tablespoons protein powder

1 cup almond milk

Instructions:

1. Place the spinach, kale, mango, strawberries, banana, flaxseed, chia seed, protein powder, and milk in the medium or large Magic Bullet blending cup. Screw on the blade assembly and place the cup on the Magic Bullet. Press down to blend until smooth, about five seconds.

2. When the Magic Bullet is finished blending, pour the shake into a glass, and enjoy.

Nutritional Info: Calories: 172, Sodium: 61 mg, Dietary Fiber: 7.4 g, Fat: 3.1 g, Carbs: 33.6 g, Protein: 6.1 g.

Dark Chocolate Protein Shake

This rich and creamy protein shake is the perfect way to get all of your vitamins and minerals for the day, but it's also the perfect way to satisfy your craving for dark chocolate.

Prep time: 2 minutes
Cook time: 2 minutes
Servings: 1

Ingredients:

1 cup almond milk

2 tablespoons cocoa powder

1 banana, peeled

3 ice cubes

6 tablespoons protein powder

1 tablespoon dark chocolate chunks

Instructions:

1. Place the almond milk, cocoa powder, banana, ice, protein powder, and chocolate chunks into the Medium Magic Bullet blending cup. Screw on the blade assembly and place the cup on the Magic Bullet. Press down to blend until smooth, about five seconds.

2. When the Magic Bullet is finished blending, pour the shake into a glass, and enjoy.

Nutritional Info: Calories: 822, Sodium: 306 mg, Dietary Fiber: 11.7 g, Fat: 60.2 g, Carbs: 48.6 g, Protein: 39.1 g.

Blueberry Almond Protein Shake

This healthy protein shake is a great way to start the day or for after a workout. Thanks to your Magic Bullet things like almonds and seeds blend to a smooth and luxurious texture.

Prep time: 2 minutes

Cook time: 2 minutes

Servings: 1

Ingredients:

1 cup almond milk

1/4 cup almonds

1/2 cup blueberries

1/4 teaspoon ground cinnamon

1 banana, peeled

1 tablespoon ground chia seeds

6 tablespoons protein powder

Instructions:

1. Place the almond milk, almonds, cinnamon, banana, chia seeds, and protein powder in the Medium Magic Bullet blending cup. Screw on the blade assembly and place the cup on the Magic Bullet. Press down to blend until smooth, about ten seconds.

2. When the Magic Bullet is finished blending, pour the shake into a glass, and enjoy.

Nutritional Info: Calories: 958, Sodium: 302 mg, Dietary Fiber: 13.4 g, Fat: 69.8 g, Carbs: 56.4 g, Protein: 42.4 g.

Carrot Coconut Protein Shake

This shake is packed with vital protein for helping to build and repairs muscles, but the best part is that it tastes just like carrot cake. Once you've tried this shake, you're going to want to make it every day.

Prep time: 2 minutes
Cook time: 2 minutes
Servings: 2

Ingredients:

4 carrots, peeled and chopped

2 cups almond milk

1/2 teaspoon vanilla extract

1 cup plain or vanilla yogurt

1/4 cup shredded coconut

1/4 cup walnuts

1/2 teaspoon ground cinnamon

1/4 teaspoon ground ginger

1/4 teaspoon ground nutmeg

1 tablespoon honey or agave syrup

Instructions:

1. Place the carrot, milk, vanilla, yogurt, coconut, walnuts, spices, and honey in the large Magic Bullet blending cup. Screw on the blade assembly and place the cup on the Magic Bullet. Press down to blend until smooth, about ten seconds.

2. When the Magic Bullet is finished blending, pour the shake into two glasses, and enjoy.

Nutritional Info: Calories: 860, Sodium: 209 mg, Dietary Fiber: 10.7 g, Fat: 71.4 g, Carbs: 46.5 g, Protein: 17.7 g.

9

SOUPS

Butternut Squash Soup

This rich and hearty Fall and Winter soup is the perfect way to warm up on a cold day. Your Magic Bullet guarantees that your butternut squash soup is always a smooth, velvety texture in seconds.

Prep time: 15 minutes

Cook time: 45 minutes

Servings: 6

Ingredients:

1 large butternut squash, peeled and chopped into large chunks

1 tablespoon butter

2 tablespoons olive oil

1/2 yellow onion, chopped

3 cloves garlic, minced

1 sprig fresh rosemary

1 sprig fresh thyme

1 quart chicken stock

Salt and black pepper

Instructions:

1. Set your oven to 450 F and place the squash on a baking sheet. Use a brush to coat the squash with olive oil and sprinkle with salt and black pepper. Place in the oven and cook until the squash is softened and slightly charred.

2. In a large saucepan, melt the butter and add the onion, garlic, rosemary, and thyme.

3. When the onion has softened, add the squash and chicken broth. Simmer until the squash is completely soft.

4. Working in batches, place the mixture into the large Magic Bullet blending cup. Screw on the blade assembly and place the cup on the Magic Bullet.

5.   Press down to blend until smooth, about ten to twenty seconds. Repeat this step until all of the soup is pureed. Served hot.

Nutritional Info: Calories: 91, Sodium: 525 mg, Dietary Fiber: 1.2 g, Fat: 7 g, Carbs: 7.4 g, Protein: 1.2 g.

Creamy Tomato and Basil Soup

This rich tomato soup is reminiscent of vibrant Italian flavors of fresh tomatoes and basil for a satisfying yet refreshing soup that works perfectly as a meal or an appetizer.

Prep time: 20 minutes

Cook time: 45 minutes

Servings: 4

Ingredients:

2 lbs. fresh Roma tomatoes

6 cloves garlic

1 yellow onion, chopped

4 tablespoons olive oil

1 can crushed tomatoes

2 cups chicken stock

1/2 cup fresh basil, chopped

1/2 cup heavy cream

Salt and Black pepper

Instructions:

1. Boil a pot of water and add the tomatoes, cooking until skins begin to burst. remove from the water, remove skins, and set aside.

2. In a large sauce pan, heat the oil and add the onion and a pinch of salt and pepper, cooking until soft.

3. Add the garlic and cook until just browned. Add the tomatoes, chicken stock, basil, and another pinch of salt and pepper. Simmer for 40 minutes.

4. Working in batches, place the mixture into the large Magic Bullet blending cup. Screw on the blade assembly and place the cup on the Magic Bullet.

5. Press down to blend until smooth, about ten to twenty seconds. Repeat this step until all of the soup is pureed. Add the cream and stir well before serving.

Nutritional Info: Calories: 236, Sodium: 401 mg, Dietary Fiber: 3.5 g, Fat: 20.4 g, Carbs: 13.8 g, Protein: 3.3 g.

Red Lentil Soup

This vegan soup is super easy to make and it's also a great way to get vitamins, nutrients, and a big dose of protein. Lentils are packed with flavor and a full complement of daily nutrition, and your Magic Bullet allows you to make perfectly creamy soup in minutes.

Prep time: 10 minutes

Cook time: 45 minutes

Servings: 6

Ingredients:

1 cup red lentils

4 cups vegetable stock

2 tablespoons olive oil

1 onion, chopped

4 cloves garlic, chopped

1/2 teaspoon ground cumin

1/2 teaspoon coriander

Salt and black pepper

Instructions:

1. In a large sauce pan, heat the oil and add the onion, cumin, and coriander. Cook until the onion is soft and the spices are fragrant. Add the garlic and cook until just browned. Add the lentils, vegetable stock, and a pinch of salt and pepper. Cook until the lentils are soft, about 30 minutes.

2. Place the mixture in the large Magic Bullet blending cup. Screw on the blade assembly and place the cup on the Magic Bullet. Press down to blend until the lentils are partially broken down. This will give you a more textured soup. For a smoother soup, blend an additional 20 to 30 seconds.

Nutritional Info: Calories: 171, Sodium: 483 mg, Dietary Fiber: 10.2 g, Fat: 6.4 g, Carbs: 23 g, Protein: 8.6 g.

Creamy Asparagus Soup

This fresh and verdant soup is perfect for entertaining in the summer or as a hearty meal on a cold winter night. Pairs perfectly with garlic and cheese croutons.

Prep time: 10 minutes
Cook time: 30 minutes
Servings: 4

Ingredients:

1 lb. fresh asparagus

2 tablespoons olive oil

1 yellow onion, chopped

4 celery stalks, chopped

1 zucchini, chopped

4 cups chicken stock

1/2 cup heavy cream

Salt and black pepper

Instructions:

1. In a large pot, heat the oil and add the onion and celery with a pinch of salt and pepper. Cook until the onion has slightly softened and add the asparagus, cooking until slightly soft. Add the zucchini and chicken stock with another pinch of salt and pepper, and simmer until all of the vegetables are soft.

2. Place the mixture in the large Magic Bullet blending cup. Screw on the blade assembly and place the cup on the Magic Bullet. Press down to blend until smooth. Add the heavy cream and blend until incorporated. Serve immediately.

Nutritional Info: Calories: 166, Sodium: 791 mg, Dietary Fiber: 3.8 g, Fat: 13.4 g, Carbs: 10.3 g, Protein: 4.5 g.

Blended Broccoli Soup

This healthy soup is also rich and delicious thanks to the power of your Magic Bullet . And it's so easy to make, you can throw it together for a healthy meal after a busy day.

Prep time: 10 minutes

Cook time: 25 minutes

Servings: 4

Ingredients:

4 cups broccoli, chopped

1/2 onion, chopped

2 tablespoons olive oil

2 celery stalks, chopped

2 cloves garlic, minced

1 sprig fresh thyme

4 cups chicken stock

1/2 cup heavy cream

Salt and black pepper

Instructions:

1. In a large pot, heat the oil and add the onion and celery with a pinch of salt and pepper. Cook until slightly softened, about 5 minutes. Add the garlic and thyme and cook until garlic has slightly browned. Add the broccoli and broth and simmer until the broccoli is tender.

2. Place the mixture in the large Magic Bullet blending cup. Screw on the blade assembly and place the cup on the Magic Bullet. Press down to blend until smooth. Add the heavy cream and blend until incorporated. Serve immediately.

Nutritional Info: Calories: 162, Sodium: 807 mg, Dietary Fiber: 2.9 g, Fat: 13.4 g, Carbs: 9.3 g, Protein: 3.9 g.

Zucchini Leek Soup

Leeks are an amazingly flavorful alternative to onions and they pair perfectly with the subtle flavor of fresh zucchini.

Prep time: 15 minutes
Cook time: 30 minutes
Servings: 4

Ingredients:

1 large leek, trimmed and chopped

2 tablespoons butter

2 large zucchinis, chopped

4 cloves garlic, chopped

2 stalks celery, chopped

4 cups chicken or vegetable stock

1 sprig fresh rosemary

Salt and black pepper

Instructions:

1. In a large pot, heat the butter and add the leek and celery with a pinch of salt and pepper. When the leeks have softened, add the zucchini, garlic, rosemary, stock, and a pinch of salt and pepper. Cook until the vegetables are all soft.

2. Place the mixture in the large Magic Bullet blending cup. Screw on the blade assembly and place the cup on the Magic Bullet. Press down to blend until smooth. Serve immediately.

Nutritional Info: Calories: 106, Sodium: 833 mg, Dietary Fiber: 2.4 g, Fat: 6.7 g, Carbs: 10.6 g, Protein: 3.3 g.

Curried Cauliflower Soup

This creamy Indian spiced soup is rich in complex flavors and full of nutrition. Your Magic Bullet Auto iO guarantees perfectly creamy soups which are always the proper texture.

Prep time: 20 minutes
Cook time: 30 minutes
Servings: 4

Ingredients:

1 large head cauliflower, chopped

4 tablespoons olive oil

1 yellow onion, chopped

2 stalks celery, chopped

2 carrots, chopped

3 cloves garlic, chopped

4 cups chicken broth

1 tablespoon garam masala powder

Salt and black pepper

Instructions:

1. Place the cauliflower on a baking sheet and brush with half of the olive oil and sprinkle with salt and pepper.

2. Heat your oven to 450F and bake the cauliflower until slightly browned.

3. In a large pot, heat the remaining olive oil and add the onion, celery, carrot, and garam masala powder. Cook until the spices are fragrant and add the cauliflower, and garlic, cooking until the garlic has slightly browned.

4. Add the chicken broth and a pinch of salt and pepper, and simmer until all of the vegetables have softened.

5. Place the mixture in the large Magic Bullet blending cup. Screw on the blade assembly and place the cup on the Magic Bullet.

6. Press down to blend until smooth. Serve immediately.

Nutritional Info: Calories: 239, Sodium: 858 mg, Dietary Fiber: 6.8 g, Fat: 15.6 g, Carbs: 18.6 g, Protein: 9.8 g.

Black Bean Soup

Subtle and earthy black beans are a great source of nutrition, and they also blend perfectly for a satisfyingly rich soup.

Prep time: 10 minutes

Cook time: 25 minutes

Servings: 4

Ingredients:

2 cans black beans, drained and rinsed

3 cups chicken stock

1 onion, chopped

1 teaspoon ground cumin

1 tablespoon olive oil

1 tablespoon chili powder

1 tablespoon fresh lime juice

1/3 cup tomato salsa

Salt and black pepper

Instructions:

1. In a large pot, heat the oil and add the onion, cooking until softened. Add the chili powder, and cumin and cook several more minutes until fragrant. Add the bean, chicken stock, salsa, and a pinch of salt and pepper. Simmer for 10 minutes.

2. Place half of the mixture in the large Magic Bullet blending cup. Screw on the blade assembly and place the cup on the Magic Bullet. Press down to blend until smooth. Serve immediately.

Nutritional Info: Calories: 112, Sodium: 672 mg, Dietary Fiber: 5.6 g, Fat: 4.4 g, Carbs: 14 g, Protein: 5.4 g.

Gazpacho

This traditional tomato and pepper soup is full of rich flavors and packs a kick of heat thanks to cayenne pepper.

Prep time: 20 minutes
Cook time: 40 minutes
Servings: 4

Ingredients:

8 tomatoes, cut in half

1 yellow bell pepper

1 red bell pepper

6 tablespoons olive oil

2 cloves garlic

2 cups white wine

1/4 cup lime juice

1 teaspoon cayenne pepper

Salt and black pepper

Instructions:

1. Coat the peppers and tomatoes with olive oil and char on the grill until lightly charred all over. Remove from the grill and set aside.

2. In a large pot, heat half the oil and add the onion and garlic, cooking until soft. Add the wine and reduce until most of the wine has cooked off and add the tomatoes and peppers. Cook 20 minutes and add the lime juice and cayenne pepper.

3. Place the mixture in the large Magic Bullet blending cup. Screw on the blade assembly and place the cup on the Magic Bullet. Press down to blend until smooth. Serve immediately.

Nutritional Info: Calories: 338, Sodium: 22 mg, Dietary Fiber: 3.6 g, Fat: 21.7 g, Carbs: 16.4 g, Protein: 2.8 g.

Roasted Garlic Soup

This hearty and flavorful soup used sweet roasted garlic for a delightful blend of earthy flavors that is sure to please your friends and family.

Prep time: 60 minutes

Cook time: 30 minutes

Servings: 4

Ingredients:

5 heads garlic, tops chopped off

4 tablespoons olive oil

1/2 onion, chopped

2 carrots, chopped

4 celery stalks, chopped

6 cups beef stock

Salt and black pepper

Instructions:

1. Brush the garlic with half of the olive oil, sprinkle with salt and pepper, and place on a baking sheet. Set your oven to 325F and cook the garlic for one hour. Remove from the oven and allow to cool.

2. In a large pot, heat the remaining oil and add the onion, carrot, and celery with a pinch of salt and pepper.

3. Remove the garlic cloves from the heads and add to the pot with the beef stock. Simmer for 10 to 15 minutes.

4. Place the mixture in the large Magic Bullet blending cup. Screw on the blade assembly and place the cup on the Magic Bullet. Press down to blend until smooth. Serve immediately.

Nutritional Info: Calories: 172, Sodium: 1209 mg, Dietary Fiber: 1.4 g, Fat: 14.9 g, Carbs: 6.2 g, Protein: 4.9 g.

10

QUICK BREADS

Simple White Bread

White bread from the store is full of chemicals and preservatives, but this simple recipe shows you how to make delicious white bread at home with all natural ingredients in you Magic Bullet.

Prep time: 10 minutes
Cook time: 40 minutes
Servings: 8

Ingredients:

3 1/2 cups all-purpose flour

1 package active dry yeast

1 cup milk

1/4 cup vegetable shortening

2 tablespoons sugar

1 teaspoon salt

1 egg, beaten

Instructions:

1. In a small saucepan, combine the milk, shortening, sugar, and salt over low heat until the shortening is melted and the sugar and salt have dissolved. Remove from the heat and allow to cool.

2. In the large Magic Bullet blending cup, combine the flour and yeast. Screw on the blade assembly and place the cup on the Magic Bullet. Pulse several times.

3. Pour the milk mixture into the blender and add the egg. Pulse until the mixture comes together and forms a rough dough. Remove dough and place in a bowl. Cover with a towel and allow to rest for 45 minutes. The dough should almost double in size.

4. On a floured surface knead the dough several times and place in a greased loaf pan. Set you oven to 375F and back until the loaf is golden brown.

Nutritional Info: Calories: 293, Sodium: 314 mg, Dietary Fiber: 1.7 g, Fat: 8.2 g, Carbs: 46.6 g, Protein: 7.7 g.

French Sourdough Bread

Sourdough bread is an ancient bread that used a microbial started rather than yeast to rise, and give it it's signature tangy flavor. Try this recipe and see why bakers have been using this method for centuries.

Prep time: 1 hour
Cook time: 20 minutes
Servings: 8

Ingredients:

1 cup and 2 tablespoons bread flour

1/2 teaspoon salt

1/2 cup sourdough starter

1/4 teaspoon sugar

2.5 ounces warm water

1 tablespoons olive oil

Instructions:

1.   In the large Magic Bullet blending cup, combine the flour, salt, and sugar, and pulse to blend.

2.   Add the starter, water, and oil and pulse until a rough dough forms. Remove the dough from the blender and place on a floured surface.

3.   Fold the dough over itself 5 times, allowing to rest for a few minutes between each turn. Set aside for 40 minutes to rest.

4.   Set your oven to 425F and place the dough in an oven safe dish. Bake for 10 minutes and reset the temperature to 400 and bake an additional 20 minutes or until the loaf is browned.

5.   Remove the loaf from the oven and tap the bottom with a spoon. If it sounds hollow, it is finished. Allow to cool before slicing.

Nutritional Info: Calories: 41, Sodium: 176 mg, Dietary Fiber: 0.1 g, Fat: 1.9 g, Carbs: 5.1 g, Protein: 0.9 g.

Rye Bread

Rye bread has a unique flavor thanks to the addition of rye flour which gives it its famous earthy flavor and hearty texture.

Prep time: 25 minutes

Cook time: 40 minutes

Servings: 8

Ingredients:

1 1/4 cups bread flour

1/2 cup pumpernickel

1/3 cup potato flour

1/2 cup warm water

1 1/4 teaspoons dry active yeast

1/2 teaspoon caraway seeds

1/2 tablespoon sugar

2 tablespoons vegetable oil

Instructions:

1. In the large Magic Bullet blending cup, combine the bread flour, pumpernickel, potato flour, water, yeast. caraway seeds, sugar, and oil. Screw on the blade assembly and place the cup on the Magic Bullet. Pulse until the mixture becomes a rough dough.

2. Remove the dough from the blending cup and place on a floured surface. Knead until the dough is smooth. Place the dough in a lightly greased bowl and allow to rise until it has doubled in size.

3. Set your oven to 350F and place the dough in a loaf pan. Tent with aluminum foil and bake for 20 minutes. Remove the foil and bake an additional 20 minutes or until the top of the loaf is golden brown. Remove from the oven and allow to cool before slicing.

Nutritional Info: Calories: 139, Sodium: 32 mg, Dietary Fiber: 1.2 g, Fat: 3.7 g, Carbs: 23.2 g, Protein: 3.1 g.

Focaccia Bread

This fluffy and flavorful bread is perfect on its own or as the foundation for a sandwich. You can also top it with your favorite pizza ingredients for a fun thick crust pizza.

Prep time: 25 minutes

Cook time: 15 minutes

Servings: 6

Ingredients:

1 1/3 cups all purpose flour

1/2 teaspoon salt

1/2 teaspoon sugar

1/2 tablespoon active dry yeast

1/2 teaspoon garlic powder

1/2 teaspoon dried oregano

1/2 teaspoon dried thyme

1/2 teaspoon dried basil

2 teaspoons vegetable oil

1/2 cup water

1 tablespoon olive oil

1 tablespoon Parmesan cheese, grated

1/2 cup mozzarella cheese, grated

Instructions:

1. Place the flour, salt, sugar, yeast, garlic powder, oregano, thyme, olive oil, and water in the large Magic Bullet blending cup. Screw on the blade assembly and place the cup on the Magic Bullet. Pulse until a rough dough forms. Remove from the blending cup and place on a floured surface. Knead the dough until smooth.

2. Use the vegetable oil to coat the inside of a bowl and place the dough in the bowl. Let rest for 20 minutes.

3. Set your oven to 450F and place the dough on a greased baking dish. Form into a loaf shape and sprinkle with the cheeses. Bake for 15 minutes or until the top is golden brown.

Nutritional Info: Calories: 153, Sodium: 235 mg, Dietary Fiber: 1.1 g, Fat: 5 g, Carbs: 22.3 g, Protein: 4.5 g.

Pizza Dough

Homemade pizza is a fun activity for the whole family, and your Magic Bullet allows you to make an easy pizza dough that is perfectly flavorful and chewy.

Prep time: 10 minutes

Cook time: 5 minutes

Servings: 6

Ingredients:

3/4 cups warm water

1 package active dry yeast

2 cups all purpose flour

1 teaspoon sugar

1 teaspoon salt

3 tablespoons olive oil

Instructions:

1. Place the water and yeast in the large Magic Bullet blending cup and allow to sit at room temperature for 5 minutes.

2. Add the flour, sugar, salt, and oil, and screw on the blade assembly and place the cup on the Magic Bullet. Pulse until a rough dough forms. Remove from the blending cup and place on a floured surface. Knead the dough until it feels smooth, and place in an oiled bowl. Allow to rest for 1 hour before stretching for pizza.

Nutritional Info: Calories: 218, Sodium: 390 mg, Dietary Fiber: 1.4 g, Fat: 7.5 g, Carbs: 32.9 g, Protein: 4.8 g

11

PANCAKES AND WAFFLES

Classic Buttermilk Pancakes

This classic breakfast favorite is a rich and satisfying way to start the day. Tangy buttermilk really does make a difference, and your Magic Bullet guarantees perfectly smooth batter.

Prep time: 5 minutes

Cook time: 5 minutes

Servings: 2

Ingredients:

1 cup all purpose flour

1/2 teaspoon baking soda

1 1/2 tablespoons sugar

1 1/2 cups buttermilk

1 teaspoon baking powder

1/4 teaspoon salt

1 egg, beaten

2 tablespoons butter, melted

Instructions:

1. Place the flour, baking soda, sugar, buttermilk, baking powder, salt, egg, and melted butter in the large Magic Bullet blending cup. Screw on the blade assembly and place the cup on the Magic Bullet. Pulse several times to combine.

2. Heat your griddle to 375F. You can pour the batter directly from the blending cup to the griddle. Cook until golden brown on both sides and serve immediately.

Nutritional Info: Calories: 470, Sodium: 914 mg, Dietary Fiber: 1.8 g, Fat: 16 g, Carbs: 66.8 g, Protein: 15.4 g.

Blueberry Pancakes

This fun take on the classic pancake recipe uses fresh blueberries to create a breakfast that is sure to please the whole family.

Prep time: 5 minutes

Cook time: 5 minutes

Servings: 2

Ingredients:

1 cup all purpose flour

1/2 teaspoon baking soda

1 1/2 tablespoons sugar

1/4 cup fresh blueberries

1 1/2 cups buttermilk

1 teaspoon baking powder

1/2 teaspoon ground cinnamon

1/4 teaspoon salt

1 egg, beaten

2 tablespoons butter, melted

Instructions:

1. Place the flour, baking soda, sugar, blueberries buttermilk, baking powder, cinnamon, salt, egg, and melted butter in the large Magic Bullet blending cup. Screw on the blade assembly and place the cup on the Magic Bullet. Pulse several times to combine.

2. Heat your griddle to 375F. You can pour the batter directly from the blending cup to the griddle. Cook until golden brown on both sides and serve immediately.

Nutritional Info: Calories: 482, Sodium: 915 mg, Dietary Fiber: 2.5 g, Fat: 16 g, Carbs: 69.9 g, Protein: 15.6 g.

Cranberry Walnut Pancakes

These fun pancakes are packed with fun, tangy flavors and nutty texture thanks to dried cranberries and crushed walnuts.

Prep time: 5 minutes
Cook time: 5 minutes
Servings: 2

Ingredients:

1 cup all-purpose flour

1/2 teaspoon baking soda

1 1/2 tablespoons sugar

1 1/2 cups buttermilk

1/2 cup dried cranberries

1/2 cup walnuts, chopped

1 teaspoon baking powder

1/4 teaspoon salt

1 egg, beaten

2 tablespoons butter, melted

Instructions:

1. Place the flour, baking soda, sugar, buttermilk, cranberries, walnuts, baking powder, salt, egg, and melted butter in the large Magic Bullet blending cup. Screw on the blade assembly and place the cup on the Magic Bullet. Pulse several times to combine.

2. Heat your griddle to 375F. You can pour the batter directly from the blending cup to the griddle. Cook until golden brown on both sides and serve immediately.

Nutritional Info: Calories: 679, Sodium: 915 mg, Dietary Fiber: 4.9 g, Fat: 34.4 g, Carbs: 72.4 g, Protein: 23 g.

Buckwheat Pancakes

If you're looking for a way to get more whole grains in your pancakes, these traditional buckwheat pancakes are sure to hit the spot and provide a little extra nutrition.

Prep time: 10 minutes

Cook time: 5 minutes

Servings: 2

Ingredients:

1 cup buckwheat flour

1 1/2 teaspoon sugar

1 teaspoon baking powder

1/4 teaspoon salt

1/4 teaspoon baking soda

1 1/4 cups buttermilk

1 egg, beaten

1/4 teaspoon vanilla extract

Instructions:

1. Place the buckwheat flour, baking soda, sugar, buttermilk, vanilla, baking powder, salt, and egg. in the large Magic Bullet blending cup. Screw on the blade assembly and place the cup on the Magic Bullet. Pulse several times to combine. Allow mixture to rest for 5 minutes before cooking.

2. Heat your griddle to 375F. You can pour the batter directly from the blending cup to the griddle. Cook until golden brown on both sides and serve immediately.

Nutritional Info: Calories: 309, Sodium: 650 mg, Dietary Fiber: 6.1 g, Fat: 5.4 g, Carbs: 54.1 g, Protein: 15.4 g.

Belgian Waffles

The decadent Belgian waffle is a classic breakfast staple, and this recipe will show you how to make perfectly golden waffles at home using your Magic Bullet.

Prep time: 10 minutes

Cook time: 5 minutes

Servings: 2

Ingredients:

1 cup all-purpose flour

1/2 teaspoon salt

2 teaspoons baking powder

1 tablespoons sugar

1 egg, beaten

3/4 cups warm milk

2 tablespoons butter, melted

1/2 teaspoon vanilla extract

Instructions:

1. Place the flour, salt, baking powder, sugar, egg, milk, butter, and vanilla into the large Magic Bullet Blending cup. Screw on the blade assembly and place the cup on the Magic Bullet. Pulse several times to combine.

2. Heat your waffle iron. You can pour the batter directly from the blending cup to the waffle iron. Cook until golden brown on both sides and serve immediately.

Nutritional Info: Calories: 437, Sodium: 743 mg, Dietary Fiber: 1.8 g, Fat: 16.2 g, Carbs: 60.9 g, Protein: 12.4 g.

Cinnamon Toast Waffles

This twist on classic Belgian waffles is a great way to have a fun breakfast on special occasions. Your Magic Bullet ensures perfectly blended batter in no time.

Prep time: 10 minutes

Cook time: 5 minutes

Servings: 3

Ingredients:

1 cup all-purpose flour

3 tablespoons spoon sugar

2 teaspoons baking powder

1/2 teaspoon salt

3/4 cups milk

1 egg, beaten

1/2 teaspoon vanilla extract

2 tablespoons brown sugar

1 teaspoon ground cinnamon

2 tablespoons butter, melted

Instructions:

1. Place the flour, 1 tablespoon of sugar, baking powder, salt, milk, egg, vanilla extract, and half teaspoon of cinnamon in the large Magic Bullet blending cup. Screw on the blade assembly and place the cup on the Magic Bullet. Pulse until smooth.

2. Heat your waffle iron and pour one third of the batter onto the iron. In a small bowl, combine the remaining sugar and cinnamon. Remove the waffle from the iron when golden brown and brush with melted butter. Sprinkle the waffles with the cinnamon and sugar mixture and serve immediately.

Nutritional Info: Calories: 316, Sodium: 467 mg, Dietary Fiber: 1.6 g, Fat: 10.8 g, Carbs: 47.1 g, Protein: 8.3 g.

Whole Wheat Waffles

This healthier alternative to traditional Belgian waffles uses whole wheat flour and oats to produce a waffle that is packed with whole grain nutrition as well as delightful flavor.

Prep time: 5 minutes

Cook time: 5 minutes

Servings: 3

Ingredients:

1/2 cup whole wheat flour

1/2 cup all-purpose flour

1/2 cup oat flour

3 tablespoons sugar

1 1/2 teaspoon baking powder

1/4 teaspoon salt

1 egg, beaten

3/4 cups milk

1 tablespoon vegetable oil

1/2 teaspoon vanilla extract

Instructions:

1. Place the whole wheat flour, all-purpose flour, oat flour, sugar, baking powder, salt, egg, milk, vegetable oil, and vanilla in the large Magic Bullet blending cup. Screw on the blade assembly and place the cup on the Magic Bullet. Pulse until the mixture is smooth.

2. Heat your waffle iron and pour on third of the mixture onto the iron. Cook until golden brown.

Nutritional Info: Calories: 353, Sodium: 246 mg, Dietary Fiber: 2.7 g, Fat: 8.7 g, Carbs: 58.7 g, Protein: 10.2 g.

Banana Waffles

These waffles let you use those bananas that are a little too brown and a little too soft to make delicious banana infused waffles that are sure to excite the entire family.

Prep time: 10 minutes
Cook time: 5 minutes
Servings: 3

Ingredients:

1 1/2 cups all-purpose flour

1/2 tablespoon baking powder

1/4 teaspoon salt

3/4 cups milk

1/2 cup ripe banana, mashed

1/4 cup vegetable oil

1 egg, beaten

1/4 teaspoon vanilla extract

Instructions:

1. Place the flour, baking powder, salt, milk, vegetable oil, egg, and vanilla extract into the large Magic Bullet blending cup. Screw on the blade assembly and place the cup on the Magic Bullet. Pulse until the mixture is smooth, then add the banana. Pulse several more times, until the banana is combined with the batter, but there are still lumps of banana.

2. Heat your waffle iron and pour on the batter. Cook until golden brown and serve immediately.

Nutritional Info: Calories: 465, Sodium: 247 mg, Dietary Fiber: 2.4 g, Fat: 21.6 g, Carbs: 57.7 g, Protein: 10.6 g.

French Toast Waffles

This fun spin on classic French toast is perfect because you get all the rich goodness of French toast but with the crunchy bite of a waffle as well.

Prep time: 10 minutes

Cook time: 5 minutes

Servings: 4

Ingredients:

1/2 cup milk

2 eggs

1/2 teaspoon vanilla extract

1/2 teaspoon salt

4 thick slices brioche bread

1/2 teaspoon ground cinnamon

Instructions:

1. Place the milk, eggs, vanilla, salt, and cinnamon in the small or Medium Magic Bullet blending cup. Screw on the blade assembly and place the cup on the Magic Bullet. Pulse until mixture is smooth and eggs are completely beaten.

2. Pour the mixture into a pan and soak the pieces of brioche, allowing them to become well saturated.

3. Heat your waffle iron and place the bread onto the iron. Press down and cook until golden brown.

Nutritional Info: Calories: 256, Sodium: 336 mg, Dietary Fiber: 1.2 g, Fat: 14.3 g, Carbs: 21.7 g, Protein: 9 g.

Chocolate Waffles

These chocolate waffles are perfect for a special breakfast or as a rich and satisfying dessert.

Prep time: 15 minutes

Cook time: 10 minutes

Servings: 2

Ingredients:

1 cup all-purpose flour

3 tablespoons sugar

1 teaspoon baking powder

1/4 teaspoon salt

1/4 cup butter

1/4 cup semi sweet chocolate chips

1/2 cup milk

1 egg

1/2 teaspoon vanilla extract

Instructions:

1. Place the butter and chocolate chips into a microwave-safe bowl. Cook for 1 minute, then stir. Continue to cook for 15 seconds at a time, stirring each time until chocolate is melted and smooth.

2. Place the flour, sugar, baking powder, salt, milk, egg, and vanilla extract in the large Magic Bullet blending cup. Add the chocolate mixture. Screw on the blade assembly and place the cup on the Magic Bullet. Pulse until smooth.

3. Heat your waffle iron and pour on the batter. Cook until slightly browned.

Nutritional Info: Calories: 686, Sodium: 517 mg, Dietary Fiber: 1.8 g, Fat: 33.1 g, Carbs: 85.2 g, Protein: 13 g.

12

NUT BUTTERS

Basic Peanut Butter

Why buy store bought peanut butter that is loaded with sugar and preservatives when you can make your own, all natural peanut butter, at home in moments with your Magic Bullet.

Prep time: 10 minutes

Cook time: 15 minutes

Servings: 12

Ingredients:

2 cups raw peanuts

1 teaspoon salt

1 tablespoon vegetable oil

1 teaspoon honey or agave syrup

Instructions:

1. Heat your oven to 350F and spread the peanuts on a baking sheet. Roast the nuts in the oven until just toasted, about 10 minutes.

2. Place the peanuts in the large Magic Bullet blending cup and pulse to finely chop the nuts. Add the oil, salt, and honey, and blend until you have reached your ideal consistency. The longer your blend the smoother your peanut butter will be.

Nutritional Info: Calories: 150, Sodium: 198 mg, Dietary Fiber: 2.1 g, Fat: 13.1 g, Carbs: 4.4 g, Protein: 6.3 g.

Almond Butter

This nutritious alternative to traditional peanut butter is made creamy and smooth thanks to the powerful processing from your Magic Bullet.

Prep time: 5 minutes
Cook time: 15 minutes
Servings: 12

Ingredients:

2 cups raw unsalted almonds

2 to 3 tablespoons vegetable oil

Instructions:

1. Heat your oven to 350F and spread the almonds on a baking sheet. Roast the nuts in the oven until just toasted, about 10 minutes.

2. Place the peanuts in the large Magic Bullet blending cup. Screw on the blade assembly and place the cup on the Magic Bullet. Pulse to finely chop the nuts. Continue pulsing until you have reached your desired consistency.

Nutritional Info: Calories: 112, Sodium: 0 mg, Dietary Fiber: 2 g, Fat: 10.2 g, Carbs: 3.4 g, Protein: 3.4 g.

Chocolate Pecan Butter

This delicious spread is perfect for toast or making a fun batch of pancakes or waffles. You can try substituting other nuts for interesting flavor combinations.

Prep time: 5 minutes

Cook time: 15 minutes

Servings: 12

Ingredients:

2 cups raw pecans

1 oz. dark chocolate, chopped

1/2 tablespoon cocoa powder

1/4 teaspoon salt

Instructions:

1. Heat your oven to 350F and spread the pecans on a baking sheet. Roast the nuts in the oven until just toasted, about 5 to 7 minutes.

2. Place the toasted nuts into the large Magic Bullet blending cup and add the chocolate, cocoa powder, and salt. Blend until the nuts have broken down and the mixture becomes smooth.

Nutritional Info: Calories: 208, Sodium: 52 mg, Dietary Fiber: 3.2 g, Fat: 20.7 g, Carbs: 5.5 g, Protein: 3.2 g.

Pumpkin Walnut Butter

This fun nut butter is great in the fall or any time you want to enjoy the warm comforting flavors of pumpkin and nuts.

Prep time: 5 minutes
Cook time: 15 minutes
Servings: 12

Ingredients:

2 cups raw walnuts

1/3 cup pumpkin puree

1/2 teaspoon ground cinnamon

1/2 teaspoon ground nutmeg

1/4 teaspoon ground cloves

Instructions:

1. Heat your oven to 350F and spread the walnuts on a baking sheet. Roast the nuts in the oven until just toasted, about 10 minutes.

2. Place the nuts, pumpkin, and spices into the large Magic Bullet blending cup. Screw on the blade assembly and place the cup on the Magic Bullet. Pulse to finely chop the nuts. Continue pulsing until you have reached your desired consistency.

Nutritional Info: Calories: 132, Sodium: 1 mg, Dietary Fiber: 1.7 g, Fat: 12.4 g, Carbs: 2.8 g, Protein: 5.1 g.

Sunflower Seed Butter

This healthy seed butter goes well on toast, with yogurt, and with fruit. It's also the perfect alternative to nut butters for those with nut allergies.

Prep time: 10 minutes

Cook time: 15 minutes

Servings: 12

Ingredients:

2 cups sunflower seeds

3 tablespoons sugar

2 tablespoons coconut oil, melted

1/4 teaspoon salt

1/2 teaspoon cinnamon

1 teaspoon vanilla extract

Instructions:

1. Heat your oven to 350F and spread the sunflower seeds on a baking sheet. Roast the seeds in the oven until just toasted, about 10 minutes.

2. Place the sugar into the large Magic Bullet blending cup. Screw on the blade assembly and place the cup on the Magic Bullet. Pulse until the sugar becomes a powder. Then add the seeds, coconut oil, salt, cinnamon, and vanilla. Continue blending until the seeds break down into a creamy butter.

Nutritional Info: Calories: 77, Sodium: 51 mg, Dietary Fiber: 0.7 g, Fat: 6.2 g, Carbs: 4.7 g, Protein: 1.6 g.

13

CONDIMENTS AND DRESSINGS

Classic Mayonnaise

Right behind ketchup, mayonnaise is the most popular condiment in the United States because it adds just the right amount of flavor and moisture to everything. Making your own mayonnaise at home with your Magic Bullet means you get the creamiest, most flavorful mayo in the world.

Prep time: 5 minutes

Cook time: 5 minutes

Servings: 12

Ingredients:

2 egg yolks

1 tablespoon lemon juice

2 teaspoons white wine or white vinegar

1 teaspoon dijon mustard

1 teaspoon salt

1 cup canola oil

Instructions:

1. Place the egg yolks, lemon juice, vinegar, mustard, and salt in the large Magic Bullet blending cup. Screw on the blade assembly and place the cup on the Magic Bullet. Blend until the mixture is smooth and creamy, about 30 seconds.

2. Unscrew the blade assembly and drizzle in a couple of teaspoons of oil and replace the blade assembly. Blend until smooth. Repeat this until all of the oil is used.

Nutritional Info: Calories: 171, Sodium: 200 mg, Dietary Fiber: 0 g, Fat: 19 g, Carbs: 0.2 g, Protein: 0.5 g.

Homemade Tomato Ketchup

The classic staple of American tables, tomato ketchup is actually pretty easy to make, and thanks to your Magic Bullet blender, you will get perfectly blended ketchup in no time.

Prep time: 10 minutes

Cook time: 1 hour

Servings: 24

Ingredients:

1 14 oz. can crushed tomatoes

1/4 cup water

1/3 cup sugar

1/3 cup white vinegar

1/2 teaspoon onion powder

1/4 teaspoon garlic powder

1 teaspoon salt

1/8 teaspoon celery salt

1/8 teaspoon mustard powder

1/4 teaspoon black pepper

Instructions:

1. In a medium saucepan over medium heat, cook the tomatoes for approximately 45 minutes.

2. Place the tomatoes in the large Magic Bullet blending cup with the water, sugar, vinegar, onion powder, garlic powder, salt, celery salt, mustard, and pepper. Screw on the blade assembly and place the cup on the Magic Bullet and blend until smooth.

Nutritional Info: Calories: 18, Sodium: 129 mg, Dietary Fiber: 0.5 g, Fat: 0 g, Carbs: 4.2 g, Protein: 0.4 g.

Spicy Ketchup

Looking for a fun way to kick up the flavor of your traditional ketchup? This recipe shows you how to make a spicy ketchup that goes perfectly with burger, seafood, and of course, french fries.

Prep time: 2 minutes

Cook time: 2 minutes

Servings: 12

Ingredients:

1 cup traditional ketchup

1 teaspoon cayenne pepper

2 teaspoons brown sugar

1 tablespoon Worcestershire sauce

1 tablespoon horseradish

1/4 teaspoon garlic powder

1/4 teaspoon salt

Instructions:

1. Place the ketchup, cayenne pepper, sugar, Worcestershire sauce, horseradish, garlic, and salt, in the large Magic Bullet blending cup. Screw on the blade assembly and place the cup on the Magic Bullet and blend until smooth.

Nutritional Info: Calories: 24, Sodium: 291 mg, Dietary Fiber: 0.2 g, Fat: 0.1 g, Carbs: 6 g, Protein: 0.4 g.

Whole Grain Balsamic Dressing

Perfect for nearly any type of salad, this dressing also works as a great way to add flavor to sliced apples or pears for a fun tangy snack.

Prep time: 2 minutes
Cook time: 2 minutes
Servings: 12

Ingredients:

> *1/2 cup olive oil*
>
> *1/2 cup balsamic vinegar*
>
> *2 tablespoons lemon juice*
>
> *2 tablespoons whole grain mustard*
>
> *1/2 teaspoon ground black pepper*

Instructions:

1. Place the olive oil vinegar, lemon juice, mustard, and pepper in the large Magic Bullet blending cup. Screw on the blade assembly and place the cup on the Magic Bullet and blend until smooth.

Nutritional Info: Calories: 77, Sodium: 12 mg, Dietary Fiber: 0 g, Fat: 8.5 g, Carbs: 0.4 g, Protein: 0 g.

Honey Mustard

This fun, classic honey mustard is so versatile, you can use it as a salad dressing or as a dipping sauce for almost anything. The amazing blending power of the Magic Bullet ensures perfectly smooth honey mustard in seconds.

Prep time: 2 minutes

Cook time: 2 minutes

Servings: 12

Ingredients:

1 cup mayonnaise

4 tablespoons yellow mustard

2 tablespoon dijon mustard

4 tablespoons honey

1 tablespoon lemon juice

Instructions:

1. In the medium or large Magic Bullet blending cup, combine the mayo, mustards, honey, and lemon juice. Screw on the blade assembly and place the cup on the Magic Bullet and pulse until smooth.

Nutritional Info: Calories: 102, Sodium: 219 mg, Dietary Fiber: 0.2 g, Fat: 6.8 g, Carbs: 10.8 g, Protein: 0.4 g.

Classic Caesar Dressing

One of the most famous salads in the world, Caesar dressing comes in many variations, but this classic Caesar is modeled after the original and is guaranteed to be rich, creamy, and flavorful.

Prep time: 5 minutes

Cook time: 2 minutes

Servings: 6

Ingredients:

1/2 cup extra virgin olive oil

1/4 cup fresh lemon juice

1/2 cup Parmesan cheese, finely grated

3 anchovy filets

1 egg yolk

1 teaspoon freshly ground black pepper

Instructions:

1. Place the olive oil, lemon juice, Parmesan cheese, anchovies, egg yolk, and black pepper in the medium or large Magic Bullet blending cup. Screw on the blade assembly and place the cup on the Magic Bullet and pulse until the anchovy has broken down completely.

Nutritional Info: Calories: 102, Sodium: 219 mg, Dietary Fiber: 0.2 g, Fat: 6.8 g, Carbs: 10.8 g, Protein: 0.4 g.

Authentic Italian Dressing

Italian dressing may be an Italian-American invention, but this versatile dressing is perfect for salads and classic sandwiches.

Prep time: 2 minutes
Cook time: 2 minutes
Servings: 12

Ingredients:

1/2 tablespoon garlic powder

2 1/2 tablespoons salt

1 tablespoon onion powder

1 tablespoon sugar

2 tablespoons dried oregano

1 teaspoon black pepper

1/4 teaspoon dried thyme

1 teaspoon dried basil

1 tablespoon dried parsley

1/4 teaspoon celery salt

1/4 cup white vinegar

2/3 cup vegetable oil

2 tablespoons water

Instructions:

1. In a small bowl, mix together the garlic powder, salt, onion powder, sugar, oregano, pepper, thyme, basil, parsley, and celery salt. This mixture will make approximately 12 to 15 batches of dressing.

2. To complete the dressing, place 2 tablespoons of the dried mixture in the medium or large Magic Bullet blending cup with 1/4 cup white vinegar, 2/3 cup vegetable oil, and 2 tablespoons of water. Screw on the blade assembly and place the cup on the Magic Bullet and pulse until the ingredients are well combined.

Nutritional Info: Calories: 118, Sodium: 1145 mg, Dietary Fiber: 0.5 g, Fat: 12.2 g, Carbs: 2.4 g, Protein: 0.2 g.

Balsamic Vinaigrette

This easy and flavorful dressing is perfect for salads as well as dressing sandwiches or as a dip for bread. Once you've tried this dressing, you will find you can use it for adding a kick of flavor to almost anything.

Prep time: 5 minutes

Cook time: 2 minutes

Servings: 12

Ingredients:

1/2 cup extra virgin olive oil

1/2 cup balsamic vinegar

2 tablespoon white vinegar

1 clove garlic

1 teaspoon dijon mustard

1/4 teaspoon salt

1/2 teaspoon black pepper

Instructions:

1. Place the olive oil, vinegars, garlic, mustard, salt, and pepper, into the medium or large Magic Bullet blending cup. Screw on the blade assembly and place the cup on the Magic Bullet and pulse until the oil and vinegar are well combined.

2. You can store unused dressing directly in the blending cup and give it a quick pulse to recombine after storing.

Nutritional Info: Calories: 75, Sodium: 56 mg, Dietary Fiber: 0 g, Fat: 8.4 g, Carbs: 0.3 g, Protein: 0.1 g.

Cilantro Lime Dressing

This tangy lime based dressing adds the fresh and powerful flavor of cilantro for a dressing that is perfect for salads or as a fresh tasting condiment for tacos and sandwiches.

Prep time: 2 minutes

Cook time: 2 minutes

Servings: 12

Ingredients:

1 clove garlic

1 Jalapeño pepper, seeds removed

1 teaspoon fresh ginger, grated

1/4 cup fresh lime juice

1/3 cup honey or agave syrup

2 teaspoons balsamic vinegar

1/4 cup cilantro leaves, chopped

1/2 cup olive oil

Instructions:

1. Place the garlic, Jalapeño, ginger, lime juice, honey, vinegar, cilantro, and olive oil in the large Magic Bullet blending cup. Screw on the blade assembly and place the cup on the Magic Bullet and pulse until the ingredients are well combined.

Nutritional Info: Calories: 102, Sodium: 1 mg, Dietary Fiber: 0.1 g, Fat: 8.4 g, Carbs: 8.1 g, Protein: 0.1 g.

14

SAUCES

Pizza Sauce

Believe it or not, many of the world's greatest pizza sauces are not cooked prior to making pizza. Because you are going to bake the pizza, a raw sauce maintains the fresh flavor of raw tomatoes for a truly classic and memorable taste.

Prep time: 5 minutes

Cook time: 2 minutes

Servings: 4

Ingredients:

1 can tomato paste

6 oz. warm water

3 tablespoon Parmesan cheese, finely grated

1 teaspoon garlic powder

1 tablespoon sugar

1 teaspoon anchovy paste

1 teaspoon onion powder

1/2 teaspoon dried oregano

1/4 teaspoon dried basil

Salt and black pepper

Instructions:

1. Place the tomato paste, water, Parmesan cheese, garlic, sugar, anchovy, onion, oregano, basil, and a pinch of salt and black pepper in the medium or large Magic Bullet blending cup. Screw on the blade assembly and place the cup on the Magic Bullet and pulse until the ingredients are well combined.

Nutritional Info: Calories: 69, Sodium: 174 mg, Dietary Fiber: 1.9 g, Fat: 3.2 g, Carbs: 12.2 g, Protein: 3.7 g.

Tzatziki Sauce

This traditional fresh flavored Greek sauce can be used for so many things because it has such a mild yet distinctive flavor. Use it as a dip, a dressing for salads and sandwiches, and so much more.

Prep time: 5 minutes
Cook time: 5 Minutes
Servings: 12

Ingredients:

16 oz. plain Green Yogurt

1 cucumber, peeled and grated

1 clove garlic, finely minced

1 tablespoon lemon juice

1 tablespoon parsley, finely chopped

1 tablespoon fresh dill, finely chopped

Salt and black pepper

Instructions:

1. Place the yogurt, cucumber, garlic, lemon juice, parsley, and dill in the large Magic Bullet blending cup. Screw on the blade assembly and place the cup on the Magic Bullet and pulse several times until the ingredients are well combined. Season with salt and pepper and enjoy.

Nutritional Info: Calories: 34, Sodium: 23 mg, Dietary Fiber: 0.2 g, Fat: 0.8 g, Carbs: 2.9 g, Protein: 4.1 g.

Hollandaise Sauce

Simple, tangy, and creamy, Hollandaise sauce is best known as a topping for eggs Benedict, but once you've tried this homemade Hollandaise, you will want to top all kinds of dishes with it. You're Magic Bullet guarantees your Hollandaise is perfectly creamy every time.

Prep time: 5 minutes

Cook time: 10 minutes

Servings: 12

Ingredients:

1 cup butter, melted

3 egg yolks

1/4 teaspoon white pepper

1/2 teaspoon salt

1 tablespoon lemon juice

Instructions:

1. Place the egg yolks, salt, pepper, and lemon juice in the medium or large Magic Bullet blending cup. Screw on the blade assembly and place the cup on the Magic Bullet and pulse several times until the ingredients are well combined. Open the blending cup and drizzle in a small amount of melted butter. Screw the blades back on and blend again. Repeat this step until all of the butter has been used.

Nutritional Info: Calories: 150, Sodium: 208 mg, Dietary Fiber: 0 g, Fat: 16.5 g, Carbs: 0.2 g, Protein: 0.8 g.

Old Fashioned Horseradish Sauce

Tangy and full of flavor, this classic English horseradish sauce is the perfect accompaniment to nearly any beef dish. From London broil to tender filet mignon, this sauce will add a complex flavor that elevates your meal.

Prep time: 2 minutes

Cook time: 2 minutes

Servings: 8

Ingredients:

3 tablespoons mayonnaise

2 tablespoon spicy horseradish

1 tablespoon apple cider vinegar

1 teaspoon ground mustard

1/2 cup sour cream

1/4 teaspoon black pepper

Instructions:

1. Place the mayonnaise, horseradish, vinegar, mustard, sour cream, and pepper, in the 18 or Medium Magic Bullet blending cup. Screw on the blade assembly and place the cup on the Magic Bullet and pulse several times until the ingredients are well combined.

Nutritional Info: Calories: 56, Sodium: 56 mg, Dietary Fiber: 0.1 g, Fat: 5 g, Carbs: 2.6 g, Protein: 0.6 g.

Steak Sauce

This fun take on classic steak sauce is zesty and flavorful, and goes well on so much more than steak. Try it as a dip for fries and chips, or a tangy alternative to ketchup.

Prep time: 2 minutes

Cook time: 2 minutes

Servings: 8

Ingredients:

1 cup ketchup

2 tablespoon yellow mustard

2 tablespoon Worcestershire sauce

2 tablespoon apple cider vinegar

5 drops tabasco or Tapatio sauce

1/2 teaspoon salt

1/2 teaspoon black pepper

Instructions:

1. Place the ketchup, mustard, Worcestershire sauce, vinegar, hot sauce, salt, and pepper into the small or Medium Magic Bullet blending cup. Screw on the blade assembly and place the cup on the Magic Bullet and pulse several times until the ingredients are well combined.

Nutritional Info: Calories: 37, Sodium: 646 mg, Dietary Fiber: 0.3 g, Fat: 0.3 g, Carbs: 8.6 g, Protein: 0.7 g.

Classic Pesto Sauce

This Italian favorite is perfect for most types of pasta and it has such a rich, verdant flavor that you will want to make it all the time. Your Magic Bullet ensures that your pesto is blended perfectly evenly for optimal flavor and texture.

Prep time: 5 minutes

Cook time: 2 minutes

Servings: 12

Ingredients:

3 cups fresh basil, chopped

1 cup extra virgin olive oil

1/2 cup pine nuts

1 cup Parmesan cheese, grated

3 cloves garlic, finely minced

Instructions:

1. Place the basil, and 1 tablespoon of olive oil in the large Magic Bullet blending cup. Screw on the blade assembly and place the cup on the Magic Bullet and pulse several times until well combined. Remove the blades and the pine nuts, Parmesan cheese, and garlic. Screw on the blade assembly and place the cup on the Magic Bullet and pulse several times until the ingredients are well combined.

Nutritional Info: Calories: 200, Sodium: 44 mg, Dietary Fiber: 0.3 g, Fat: 21.7 g, Carbs: 1.3 g, Protein: 2.5 g.

15

DESSERTS

Chocolate Hazelnut Spread

Let's be honest, who can resist the signature flavor of chocolate and hazelnuts. This spread is perfect on bread, or as a filling in a fancy pastry. Once you've made this spread yourself, you will never be tempted to spend big bucks on store bought spread ever again.

Prep time: 10 minutes
Cook time: 20 minutes
Servings: 12

Ingredients:

1 cup hazelnuts

12 oz. milk chocolate, chopped

2 tablespoons vegetable oil

3 tablespoons powdered sugar

1 tablespoon cocoa powder

1/2 teaspoon vanilla extract

1/2 teaspoon salt

Instructions

1. Set your oven to 350F. Spread the hazelnuts on a baking sheet and bake for 10 to 12 minutes, or until slightly browned. Remove from the oven and set aside.

2. Place the chocolate in a microwave safe dish and cook in the microwave until melted.

3. Place the hazelnuts, oil, sugar, cocoa powder, and vanilla in the large Magic Bullet blending cup. Screw on the blade assembly and place the cup on the Magic Bullet and blend until the nuts form a paste. Add the chocolate and blend until a smooth paste forms.

Nutritional Info: Calories: 220, Sodium: 119 mg, Dietary Fiber: 1.7 g, Fat: 14.5 g, Carbs: 20.1 g, Protein: 3.2 g.

Pineapple Whip

This fresh and simple dessert has been around for decades because of how easy and delicious it is. Thanks to your Magic Bullet , you can make a perfectly smooth pineapple whip that is sure to please the entire family.

Prep time: 2 minutes
Cook time: 2 minutes
Servings: 4

Ingredients:

1 pineapple, peeled chopped and frozen

2 tablespoons honey or agave syrup

1 cup almond milk

Instructions:

1. Make sure your pineapple is completely frozen before you start. Place the pineapple chunks, honey, and almond milk into the large Magic Bullet blending cup. You may need to make several batches depending on the size of your pineapple.

2. Screw on the blade assembly and place the cup on the Magic Bullet and pulse several times until the ingredients are well combined and smooth. You may need to use a little extra almond milk to achieve your desired consistency.

Nutritional Info: Calories: 190, Sodium: 10 mg, Dietary Fiber: 1.9 g, Fat: 14.4 g, Carbs: 17.4 g, Protein: 1.6 g.

Blueberry Sorbet

The great thing about your Magic Bullet is that you can make amazing dessert treats like sorbet without the use of an ice cream maker. Because your Magic Bullet has such a powerful motor, it can easily make all kinds of fruit sorbets in minutes.

Prep time: 2 minutes

Cook time: 5 minutes

Servings: 4

Ingredients:

2 cups frozen blueberries

1/4 cup lemon juice

1/4 cup almond milk

1/3 cup honey or agave syrup

Instructions:

1. Place the blueberries, lemon juice, almond milk, and honey in the large Magic Bullet blending cup.

2. Screw on the blade assembly and place the cup on the Magic Bullet and pulse several times until the ingredients are well combined and smooth. Immediately transfer the contents of the blending cup to a glass or metal bowl and place in the freezer to firm up before serving.

Nutritional Info: Calories: 166, Sodium: 7 mg, Dietary Fiber: 2.2 g, Fat: 4 g, Carbs: 34.9 g, Protein: 1.1 g.

Banana Coconut Sorbet

This delightfully light tropical dessert is perfect any time you want to escape to the islands for a moment and indulge in a surprisingly healthy dessert treat. Perfect for when the kids want ice cream but you would rather they eat fruit instead.

Prep time: 2 minutes

Cook time: 5 minutes

servings: 4

Ingredients:

4 bananas, peeled

1/2 cup agave syrup

1 cup coconut milk

Instructions:

1. Place the bananas, coconut milk, and agave syrup into the large Magic Bullet blending cup.

2. Screw on the blade assembly and place the cup on the Magic Bullet and pulse several times until the ingredients are well combined and smooth. Immediately transfer the contents of the blending cup to a glass or metal bowl and place in the freezer to firm up before serving.

Nutritional Info: Calories: 369, Sodium: 38 mg, Dietary Fiber: 4.4 g, Fat: 14.7 g, Carbs: 63.4 g, Protein: 2.7 g.

Carrot Cake Pudding

Not only is this carrot cake pudding perfectly rich and delicious, it's also an amazing vegan recipe. The combination of fresh carrots and a variety of nuts will give you the impression that you are eating a classic carrot cake, and your Magic Bullet ensures perfect texture every time.

Prep time: 5 minutes

Cook time: 5 minutes

Servings: 4

Ingredients:

2 cups carrot juice

1 cup fresh pineapple, chopped

1 cup raw cashews

2 tablespoons maple syrup

2 tablespoons raw walnuts

2 teaspoons vanilla extract

2 teaspoons ground cinnamon

1 teaspoon lemon zest, finely minced

1 teaspoon ground nutmeg

2 avocados, pitted and peeled

Instructions:

1. In the large Magic Bullet blending cup, combine the carrot juice, pineapple, cashews, maple syrup, walnuts, vanilla, cinnamon, lemon zest, and nutmeg.

2. Screw on the blade assembly and place the cup on the Magic Bullet and blend until the ingredients are well combined and smooth. This should take about 30 to 45 seconds.

3. Remove the blades and add the avocados to the mixture. 2. Screw on the blade assembly and place the cup on the Magic Bullet and pulse several times until the ingredients are well combined and smooth. If you would like to add additional spices to the mixture to

adjust the taste you can do this and pulse the mixture for several seconds to combine.

4. Place the mixture in the refrigerator to chill before serving.

Nutritional Info: Calories: 507, Sodium: 51 mg, Dietary Fiber: 10.7 g, Fat: 38.1 g, Carbs: 39.3 g, Protein: 8.9 g.

Mango Sorbet

Mango has the perfect, smooth texture to produce rich and decadent sorbet, and your Magic Bullet has the blending power to give you perfectly smooth results every time. Once you've have this sorbet, you will want to have it every day.

Prep time: 2 minutes

Cook time: 5 minutes

Servings: 4

Ingredients:

2 cups frozen mango chunks

2 bananas

1/2 cup lemon juice

1/4 cup honey

Instructions:

1. Place mango chunks, bananas, lemon juice, and honey in the large Magic Bullet blending cup.

2. Screw on the blade assembly and place the cup on the Magic Bullet and pulse several times until the ingredients are well combined and smooth. Immediately transfer the contents of the blending cup to a glass or metal bowl and place in the freezer to firm up before serving.

Nutritional Info: Calories: 174, Sodium: 8 mg, Dietary Fiber: 3 g, Fat: 0.7 g, Carbs: 43.9 g, Protein: 1.6 g.

Made in United States
North Haven, CT
26 November 2023

44556716R00105